Forgiveness

The Proven Path
From Pain To Power
In 5 Simple Steps

*Based on the Teachings of A Course in
Miracles

Rev. Jennifer McSween

"A Course in Miracles has become, over the course of the past forty-plus years, a modern spiritual classic. According to the *Course*, "Forgiveness is the key to happiness." In *True Forgiveness* Rev. Jennifer McSween deftly shows us how to turn that key so we might be truly and forever free."

—Jon Mundy, Ph.D. author of
Living A Course in Miracles
Publisher of Miracles magazine

"I love this book *True Forgiveness!* The clear and concise precepts are a reminder of how to practice true forgiveness on a constant basis. A student of *A Course in Miracles* for over 20 years, I had grasped the fundamentals of true forgiveness, but this book has shed a new light on my practice, and helped me to understand more profoundly and in more details the deeper meaning of true forgiveness. Thank you so much for this wonderful book. It will surely help many students to better understand and practice *True Forgiveness!"*

—Danielle Chabot
Management Consultant
Avid student of *A Course in Miracles* for over twenty years

"I really like this piece of work and the simplicity in which Rev. Jennifer describes the transformational process of TRUE FORGIVENESS. It is an amazing, authentic and organic look into the transformational process of True Forgiveness. Rev. Jennifer shares her personal journey and understanding of the shift that is needed to arrive at this place of *True Forgiveness.* By re-defining the concepts of "world, self, perspective and forgiveness", as some of the key elements to embarking on the journey of *forgiveness.* As a nutritional coach helping prepare menu plans for clients to attain optimal physical health, this book is a perfect menu plan to achieve an optimal connection with self and others and the food for change is *LOVE*."

—Dr. Susan Campbell-Fournel
Health – Nutrition Consultant & Coach

"Reading *True Forgiveness*, I found myself immediately thinking of the people I know who need this information, including myself. Reverend Jennifer McSween demonstrates a deep understanding of the subject as well as the application of the teachings of *A Course In Miracles* in properly addressing it. The stories she shares of her past must have been extremely cathartic, and illustrate a genuine openness, as she exposes her life and the forgiveness she was able to find. I believe reading this book and applying it's principles will greatly improve the quality of life of the reader. At the very least, it will draw your attention to new ways of looking at life, relationships, and the connection we have to each other. Thank you Jennifer for sharing your insights and life lessons, we are better for it!"

—Reverend Gregory J Bright, B.MSc.
Executive Director
Canadian International Metaphysical Ministry

ISBN-13: 978-1976425745
ISBN-10: 1976425743

All quotes from *A Course in Miracles* © are from the Second Edition, published in 1996. They are used with permission from the copyright holder and publisher, the Foundation for Inner Peace, P.O. Box 598, Mill Valley, CA 94942-0598

DEDICATION

This book is dedicated to my mother Mary, whom I've come
to recognize as my primary Forgiveness Partner, and learned
to love in the truest sense of the word—accepting you and
letting you be exactly as you are, without judgment or
conditions.

DOWNLOAD THE AUDIOBOOK
FREE!

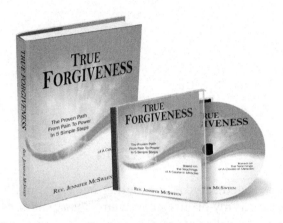

READ THIS FIRST

Just to say thanks for downloading my
book, I would like to give you the
Audiobook version 100% FREE!

TO DOWNLOAD GO TO:
http://www.subscribepage.com/audiobook

Acknowledgements

I would like to acknowledge the following people who have all been instrumental in the birth of this book in some way.

First I'd like to express my deepest love and gratitude to my loving husband Brian, who, for thirty plus years has been my moral compass, my confidante, teacher, partner and best friend. You've taught me how to laugh, and you still keep me laughing. You have supported me in every way and have always *"been there"* for me. Your eyes have always reflected a vision of me that I continually strive to be.

My beautiful daughter Jada. Thank you Baby for your patience and understanding, during the times I was not available for you, as I was writing this book. Your kind, gentle, loving and thoughtful nature is a wonderful blessing in my life and your father's. I genuinely like you, as well as love you deeply, and totally enjoy our "adventures" together. You're my true *"Ride or Die"* (smile).

I want to acknowledge and thank everyone who has attended my lectures, classes and workshops, as well as those who have used my coaching and counseling services.

I especially want to thank my Accountability Buddy, and someone who has become a dear friend, Uta Gabbay. Your keen insight and spiritual understanding often brought me clarity when I needed it most. Our mutual desire to stay true to our message, made partnering with you to write this book, feel like a sacred experience.

My deepest thanks to Revs. Robert & Mary Stoelting for writing the beautiful foreword to this book. I especially want to express my deepest love and gratitude, for your generosity, patience and loving support in helping me edit this book. I truly feel that you have both been divinely guided into my life. You have not only contributed enormously to the birth of this book, but to the idea of writing it, 15 years ago.

I would also like to extend my eternal gratitude to my wonderful Book Launch Team, for your encouragement and support in helping me to express what I feel is my purpose, in yet another form—this book. By promoting and sharing *True Forgiveness* with others, you too, are being instrumental in helping people heal—transforming their relationships and the quality of their lives.

I extend my deepest gratitude to Dr. Kenneth Wapnick, founder of the Foundation for *A Course in Miracles*, for his devotion to teaching the *Course*, and his commitment to honoring the metaphysics of the *Course*. He had the ability to present the *Course's* more abstract, profound teachings, in a simple, relatable and very often, light-hearted manner. I have found his books, audio and video recordings, to be invaluable in helping me understand, how to effectively apply the teachings of the *Course* in my everyday life.

I'm also grateful for the articles and workbook lesson commentaries by the Circle of Atonement's Robert Perry, Allen Watson and Greg Mackie on *A Course in Miracles*. They too helped to make the teachings of the *Course* relatable as well as practical.

It's your thoughts alone that cause you pain.

Nothing external to your mind can hurt or injure you

in any way.

There is no cause beyond yourself that can reach down and

bring oppression.

No one but yourself affects you.

There is nothing in the world that has the power to make

you ill or sad, weak or frail.

But it is you who have the power to dominate all things

you see by merely recognizing what you are."

W-pI.190:5.1-6

Table of Contents

Foreword

When the profound work of *A Course in Miracles* (ACIM) came into our lives in 1984, we felt a deep inner knowing that it was not a "coincidence" that this significant spiritual masterpiece came to us when it did. As we continued studying the Text and applying the instructions found in the daily lessons of the Course's Workbook for Students, we came to experience a deep inner knowing and feeling that the purpose of our lives was to apply the message of the Course daily and join with others around the world to deepen our joint commitment to this powerful, enlightening and healing practice together.

We first met Jennifer McSween years ago when she came to the Pathways of Light training center in the United States for her ministerial counselor training based on *A Course in Miracles*. We found her enthusiastic and happy nature to be magnetic and we loved her loving and helpful interactions with the group while she was with us.

Over the years Jennifer's studies with ACIM have gone deeper and deeper into the core principles of the Course and how to make it work for her as she struggled with the complexities and challenges presented in her daily life. Her practice of true forgiveness has led to a consistently loving, peaceful and happy state of mind. Over the years she felt guided to share with others what she has learned. This led to her giving workshops on true forgiveness based on *A Course in Miracles*.

We celebrate that she has now put the key content of her workshops into a beautiful book, *True Forgiveness*, that could easily serve as a companion to ACIM. In her delightful and helpful book she shares with us her personal journey of the steps she has walked through. She also explains, in a beautiful, easy to understand way, how the thought system of *A Course in Miracles* changed her life.

By sharing how it has worked in her life experience, she helps us understand the difference between *conventional forgiveness* and *true forgiveness* and how to develop the habit of applying true forgiveness in *our* lives. She delves into such areas as how to let go of anger, judgment, fear, and feeling unworthy, guilty or being a victim. She brings out key lessons from ACIM and shows us how to understand and practice them.

In her book she also shows us a new way of looking at ourselves to learn to discover and recognize our true Self, bringing us peace and happiness. She helps us maintain the right mindset by remembering that everything happens in the mind and our experience is determined by our state of mind. She also identifies three major blocks to learning and how to move past these blocks.

In another delightful section of her book, Jennifer has created a blueprint for happiness, which shows us how to practice these central lessons. She gives us a powerful set of tools to bring our minds back to truth when we forget.

We see that this insightful book will help many understand and apply the core teachings that the Course lays out for us. Both new and long-time Course students will appreciate her lively and enthusiastic way of presenting key concepts in ACIM and applying them to everyday life.

Revs. Robert & Mary Stoelting
Co-founders of Pathways of Light, a spiritual organization dedicated to healing our minds and helping people access the Inner Wisdom within that will lead us to enlightenment
www.pathwaysoflight.org.

Introductory Letter

Dear *Forgiveness Partner*,

Right now you're probably wondering: *"What is a Forgiveness Partner and why is it that I'm addressing you as one; since we most likely don't know each other and if we do, we have nothing against each other? "*

You will have the answers to those questions by the time you finish this book. You see *forgiveness*, from the perspective I'll be presenting in this book, is not about pardoning another for what they have *done wrong*, but about our recognizing each other for what we *are*.

This perspective of Forgiveness is based on the teachings of *A Course in Miracles* (ACIM). A Course in Miracles is a form of Spiritual Psychotherapy that facilitates Inner Peace, Emotional Healing, and Personal Happiness through a process of shifting your perception. This process is what *A Course in Miracles* calls *forgiveness*.

You will get the most out of this book if you temporarily put aside your current perception of *Forgiveness*, and read it with an open mind.

In the following Chapters, I will focus on the *Course's* basis for its unique perspective of forgiveness, and what it is about it that makes letting go of emotional pain and guilt through this form of *forgiveness* simple, fearless, and effective.

Before I go any further, I need to say something about the language and terminology used in *A Course in Miracles* and shared throughout the book.

A Course in Miracles holds a metaphysical perspective of life, the world, and everything that takes place in the world. This is discussed in more detail in Chapter II, but what you need to know before you start reading, is that the language and terminology used in *A Course in Miracles* is metaphorical and not to be taken literally. This means that a word or term never refers to the form of the thing, but the ***idea*** it represents or meaning it conveys.

It is important that you be mindful of this distinction as you read this book for two very important Reasons:

1) *A Course in Miracles* uses a lot of Christian/religious and psychological terminology – again within a metaphorical context. If you were to interpret the words literally, you would find what you are reading misleading or confusing; as the Religious terminology is abstract.

2) The idea of *forgiveness* is about *letting go*. Since the perspective is metaphorical, if you continue to define *forgiveness* literally you will neither be able to understand nor practice the ideas presented here.

I have included an **Appendix** at the back of this book of some of the **Key Metaphorical Terms** in *A Course in Miracles* to metaphorically *keep you on Course* as you read through it.

This Book is divided into three main parts:

PART I: A NEW PERSPECTIVE

I share some of my personal story — my journey of healing through my discovery of *A Course in Miracles'* perspective of *Forgiveness*, and the central ideas of *A Course in Miracles* that form the basis of *True Forgiveness*.

PART II: UNDERSTANDING TRUE FORGIVENESS

I talk about the problem — why we struggle — with forgiveness as it's perceived and practiced in the world; how *True Forgiveness* solves the problem, and the #1 requirement for practicing *Course based Forgiveness* or *True Forgiveness*.

PART III: PRACTICING TRUE FORGIVENESS

This section is all about putting the ideas into practice. I share the "CORE 5 STEP FORGIVENESS PROCESS," a "BLUEPRINT FOR HAPPINESS" based on the central ideas taught in the *Course*. This is a sort of Step-By-Step Guide for *living Forgiveness*, as a way of life.

I close with a Meditative Process based on the last paragraph of Chapter 16 in *A Course in Miracles*, referred to as: ***"The Forgiveness Prayer."***

As you read this book, please be mindful that there is a metaphorical meaning behind the words and ideas that you are reading. After reading this book you will never look at *"forgiveness"* in the same way again, simply because of the saying, *"you can't "un-see" or "un-know" something"*, or in the words of Ralph Waldo Emerson:

> *"One's mind, once stretched by a new idea,*
> *never returns to its original dimension."*

So turn the page, read on, and learn about the perspective and practice of *"Forgiveness"* that will bring you lasting peace, deep healing and genuine happiness...

SECTION I

A NEW PERSPECTIVE

CHAPTER I

Discovering *"True Forgiveness"*

Forgiveness is the Answer...True Forgiveness

Have you ever felt certain you had forgiven something or someone only to find yourself reliving the pain, whenever you're faced with the experience?

- Do you find yourself wondering if there was a part you did wrong?
- Are you thinking that maybe forgiving really means feeling the pain, but denying it, by pretending that the thing that you judged to be the cause of your pain didn't happen?
- Are you secretly thinking that maybe—just maybe forgiveness doesn't really work, or at least, not for you or with your specific situation...

If you've had this experience in the past or this is what you're experiencing right now, I'd like to share something with you that is guaranteed to bring you peace:

1) It's not you. You aren't doing anything wrong. You have not missed any steps.
2) You're not alone. Almost everyone struggles with practicing *forgiveness* the way it's conventionally viewed and practiced.
3) I was exactly where you are. I had the same experience and faced the same struggles. I was able to resolve them by learning and practicing a simple 5 Step Process for *True Forgiveness* that I'm going to share with you in this book.

I promise you that if you learn and apply what I'll be sharing in the coming pages, you will understand and experience "true" *forgiveness.* You will learn how to *forgive* without denying your feelings and without pain or fear that something can be unforgivable.

In September 2003, my mother came back to Montreal to live permanently after being in the US for the previous 30 years. Within a couple of months of her return we noticed she was becoming quite ill.

By February of 2004, she had a complete breakdown. Her life literally became mine and as much as I wanted to be fully present and available for her in a loving way, I found that I just couldn't do it. I was feeling hurt, disappointed, angry, resentful, and once again, abandoned by my mother.

Here's My Story

I was raised by my maternal grandmother from the age of 3 months in a little village off the ocean in Trinidad, called Matelot.

My parents were not together, however my grandmother never spoke one ill word against my father and taught me to always treat him with the same respect and obedience that I would if we had a traditional living situation. It was also not uncommon to have my father seated at our dinner table at times for Christmas or some other occasion.

He was very present in my life. As a matter of fact, I was the quintessential *Daddy's Girl.* I have a lot of fond memories of times spent with my father during childhood years. One of my earliest and nicest memories was of being around three years old when he took me to get my first pair of running shoes.

The shopkeeper was a childhood friend of my father and the place was the equivalent to a General Store that sold everything from food to fishing gear. I remember staring up excitedly at the very high counter where the shopkeeper placed two shoeboxes for my dad to make his selection.

My dad lifted me up ever so gently and sat me down on the high counter. He opened one of the boxes and took out the most beautiful little pair of running shoes I had ever seen. It was a yellow background with tiny multicolored flowers and yellow laces down the front. My dad placed one shoe on each foot and tied each lace into a bow. He looked at me with a questioning smile and asked: *"So Mamzelle...do you like them?"*

My joy was indescribable!

Growing Pains

I was baptized and raised in the Catholic branch of a religiously diverse family tree. The village of Matelot was predominantly Catholic.

The population of the village was about 1000, 800 of whom were related either through blood or belief. It was a typical little village in which everyone knew each other's business and everyone looked out for everyone else. It was not uncommon for children to be pulled up by an adult on the street, who was neither a family member nor relative, if you were caught misbehaving. And you dared not go home and complain about it. Actually, most of the time the news made it back to your home before you did and you'd then have to face those consequences too.

My grandmother was highly regarded and very involved in the church and community affairs. She was very well liked and people would frequently come to her for help or advice about their marriage, parenting problems, illness, etc. She was generous to a fault, always lending a helping hand to someone in need —on many occasions I remember delivering our last loaf of bread to a family who my grandmother heard "*didn't have any*".

She was an amazing cook. She had a great sense of style and loved to wear hats with matching handbags to church and on special occasions. There was a grace and elegance about her and she carried herself in a regal manner. Polite and courteous, she felt there was never an excuse for rudeness; and was quite the disciplinarian, though in a kind and loving way.

She was deeply religious, yet very in touch with what was going on in the world. In some ways, I thought she was a woman who was way ahead of her time as I recall how thrilled she would be whenever she heard of a woman being appointed to some position of power or authority, or excelling in a male dominated arena.

My grandmother was always caring and encouraging towards me. She strongly encouraged me to succeed academically, and led me to believe I could accomplish anything if I applied myself. She taught me to be kind and generous, to respect myself, and others, and be considerate of the feelings of others. She taught me to be honest; not to hold grudges; to forgive the people who hurt you...and of course, go to church regularly.

Except for the part about church, my grandmother's teachings are still part of the moral code by which I try to live and that I'm now passing on to my daughter.

I loved my grandmother dearly both for who she was and how she treated me.

Neither shy, nor outgoing as a child, I was somewhat of a loner, but I recall enjoying my own company – as I still do. I loved to read so I did a lot of that. Among my daily chores, was watering my grandmother's many flowerpots that lined our balcony and walkway. I created an imaginary world that existed in the flowerpots where I would interact while I watered the plants. In other words, I was neither bored nor lonely.

At school, I did pretty well. I wasn't always first in class, but I usually came within the top three. I enjoyed my days in grade school because I always liked learning and we would frequently put on variety shows in which I always had a part. My grandmother was my first speaking coach showing me how to use inflection and gestures when reciting poems on stage. For some reason though, after leaving grade school, I developed an inexplicable fear of being in front of an audience that lasted well into my adult years.

I had a relatively happy and uneventful childhood, except for a couple of incidents in my early years that, along with my relationship, or lack thereof with my mother, I processed in a painful way. Throughout my life, there always seemed to have been an undercurrent or thin thread of sadness that was woven into the fabric of my life. I didn't know it at the time, but this would be the catalyst for my interest in helping people transform their lives and the work that I now do in the area of counseling, healing, and specifically with *forgiveness*.

My childhood memories of times with my mother are few and not very fond. Both my parents lived and worked in the city, but would come to visit their respective families in the country. I have more fond memories of my father, not because he visited more frequently, but because he spent quality time with me.

I remember my mother's visits were filled with mixed emotions. She would come for weekends, arriving on a Friday night. I would always feel so happy that she had come, but knew that she wouldn't be staying long. I used to want to be with her all the time and have her take me places or do things with me like my dad would. Also, each time she visited I secretly hoped that *maybe, just maybe,* this time she would stay or take me with her when she left.

She seemed to spend most of the time sleeping and both she and my grandmother would tell me that she was tired because she was working very hard to take care of me. She would always leave Monday mornings in the wee hours before I was awake.

I would wake up on a Monday morning after one of my mother's weekend visits and run towards the entrance to her room expectantly. The bedroom in which she would stay had a closet space built in to the wall at the back of the room and closed off by a set of drapes. My mother would hang her clothes on the rack and place her shoes the floor directly beneath them.

The drapes stopped about six inches above the floor so her shoes could be seen the moment you approached the room. I would rush towards her room hoping to see her shoes on the floor beneath the drapes, because that would mean, this time she had stayed. It would be empty and I would have an immediate, sinking feeling in my chest.

When I was eight my mother left Trinidad for Canada. My grandmother told me that she was going away so that she could make a better life for me. The plan was that I would be joining her after I finished high school to further my education. The next time I saw my mother I was twelve. She and my three aunts, her sisters, two from England and the other in Montreal, came home for Christmas.

Two years later when my grandfather died she came for the funeral. The next time I saw her was when I came to Montreal at the age 18 after finishing high school, as I was told I would.

My mother had moved to the US five years earlier and I was to stay in Canada and live with my aunt and her family.

Over the years, in between my mother's visits, she and I had corresponded by letters. I always found this to be quite the ordeal. I never seemed to know what to say. I didn't feel particularly close to my mother. She's not the inquisitive type so she never really inquired as to what was going on with me. It seemed to me like I didn't matter to her and I wasn't sure that anything I would say to her really mattered. I felt somewhat abandoned by her.

My mother's absence and lack of involvement in my life in my childhood was a constant ache in my heart. I once tried sharing this with my grandmother. I don't remember her exact words and in retrospect I don't think it was her intent, but her response made me feel like I was being ungrateful. In my childlike mind, I took it to mean that my feelings didn't really matter and/or that I shouldn't have felt the way I did. I never said anything about missing my mother or my feelings again, not to my grandmother or anyone else.

Throughout my high school years, I looked forward to joining my mother after graduating as I was told I would, but at the same time I was a bit apprehensive. As I mentioned above I did not feel particularly close to my mother. When I came to Canada, I realized I didn't really know who she was as a person. I wondered if we would get along. Maybe she felt the same way and that played a part in her decision to have me live with my aunt in Canada while she lived in the US.

The relationship between us was quite strained. I found it very difficult to talk to her. Whenever I tried to tell her anything about how I felt growing up or about any of my experiences, she would become very defensive. She seemed to think I was blaming her and trying to make her feel guilty for the choices she made, and in all honesty for a period of time, there was a part of me that did.

But for the most part, I just wanted to let her know how hurt I had been feeling and that I never felt like I mattered to her. This was not intended to make her feel bad, but I was hoping she would say something that would make me feel differently. I guess that at the time, I thought that was the way to make my pain go away and mend our relationship in some way.

Well that didn't happen. As a matter of fact, I felt worse because she would get defensive about what I was saying and I would feel guilty for telling her those things. After a while I stopped. I stopped trying to tell her about anything that I found remotely troubling. I decided I would have to work it out on my own.

Letting Go of the Pain

I lived with my aunt and her family until I was 21 then I moved out on my own. I had completed college and decided to take a year off before starting University. I was not yet sure what I wanted to study.

I had been working as a Nurse's Aid at the Montreal Neurological Institute where people came to be treated for brain and spinal disorders. To this day it was my most rewarding job experience. I still don't know whether it was *because of or in spite of the fact* that it made me come to terms with my own mortality.

I was in my early twenties and when you're in your twenties you think you're going to live forever. During the summer, there were many young people, also in their twenties, being brought in as a result of diving, boating, and motorcycle accidents. Some of them suffered various forms of paralysis; brain damage that would change the way they were forever; others died shortly after. Seeing this made me feel grateful just to be able to get up and swing my legs off the bed every morning and stand on my feet on my own.

There were also elderly people, some in various stages of senility or who had brain tumors or disorders. Some of them had this sense of inner joy and gratitude regardless of what they had experienced throughout their lives, and in spite of their current condition. Others were bitter, filled with regret and/or felt that life had given them a raw deal all the way to the end. They would say things like, "my life would have been better if..." or they were, "happy until they were hurt, betrayed or disappointed by someone"; or, "such and such shouldn't have happened because they didn't deserve it. Life was so unfair."

I vowed to myself that I would not become one of those bitter, regretful people agonizing over and holding on to painful experiences. I was going to look for the good in whatever hand life dealt me.

It occurred to me that they didn't just wake up one morning in their senior years and suddenly become bitter and regretful; that had to be the result of holding onto stuff for years. So, if I didn't want to end up like them, I needed to let go of anything that made me feel bitter, resentful, or regretful. I had to *forgive*.

I realized that a primary source of bitterness and resentment for me was my mother's absence and lack of involvement in my life. I felt guilty for wanting more, when my grandmother was so encouraging and supportive. I loved my grandmother more than anything, but not having my mother "present" in my life used to make me feel like something vital was missing.

So, I decided I was going to look for what was good about my life situation.

I started by looking at the person I had become being raised by my grandmother. I realized I liked the way I had turned out. I liked my outlook on life, the values she instilled in me. During high school, I boarded with family friends who accepted, and treated me as one of their own. They included me in their lives and activities exposing me to opportunities I would not have had, had I been living with my mother. I liked the direction in which my life had gone, and I owe a debt of gratitude, to those wonderful family friends.

I also believed that, had I lived with my mother I would not have turned out the way I did. So our situation was really a good thing. As the years went by, I gradually began sharing this perspective with my mother. I prefaced sharing these thoughts and feelings with her by telling her she need not feel guilty about not having raised me. It took a while, but eventually she became less and less defensive and I thought less and less about wanting to make her feel guilty.

As time went on our relationship improved. It did not get to the point of being warm and fuzzy, but we were friendlier towards each other.

When my daughter was born I think we both began to see each other differently. I was able to view her now from the perspective of being a mother; she was seeing me in the role of a mother instead of her daughter.

My mother became the doting grandmother, wanting to be there in every way for her grandchild. I felt her attitude and approach towards me had softened and I seemed to feel understanding and compassion for her as a mother. I felt a new gentleness towards her. I actually felt I had let go of all the bitterness and resentment I had been holding towards her.

When she moved back to Montreal permanently in 2003, I was looking forward to her living close by. It would be the first time we would be living in the same country, let alone the same city since I was eight years old.

I wasn't looking for a mother figure at this point, but I was hoping we would have some sort of adult mother-daughter relationship. The last few years had been as great as they could be for us given our history. We were actually able to talk and genuinely laugh with each other.

I had been going to New York to help her with the move, and took care of setting up her apartment and arranging the move for her, to come back to Montreal.

The Discovery

That September in 2003 when my mother returned to Montreal, my daughter who had turned five in June was starting school. I had taken the first five years of her life off from pursuing my career to be at home with her. I enjoyed being at home during those years and it also turned out to give me the best of both worlds.

While being a stay-at-home-mom, I was also able to take that time to prepare myself to do exactly what I'm doing professionally today eighteen years later. During those five years was able to pursue and complete studies and training in Metaphysics and Spiritual Counseling. I became an Ordained Minister and through attending Toastmasters, overcame what at the time was a paralyzing fear of public speaking.

When my daughter was three, I became a CTM – Competent Toastmaster and within two months spoke on a public stage for the first time at an International Women's Day celebration. Once I got past the initial jitters of being in front of an audience I realized I felt completely at ease on stage and I was totally enjoying the experience. I wondered why I was ever afraid.

I was looking forward to re-establishing my professional life now that my daughter was starting school. When my mother became ill and her life became mine I felt I had sent off one five-year old only to be replaced by another.

She was hospitalized, observed, and examined. It was discovered that she had suffered a series of small strokes in the past that led to some damage in higher-level brain functioning. The prognosis was that she could get worse or stay the same, but she would not return to the way she used to be. This meant that she would no longer be able to live on her own and she needed to be admitted to a facility to get the professional medical care she needed.

It had been less than six months since her return and setting her up in her new place and I had to dismantle her apartment, moving most of her things into my home. Plus, I had the added responsibility of managing her personal affairs.

My mother's condition made her withdrawn, uncommunicative, distrusting, and at times even hostile. She seemed fragile, frightened, and alone. I was hurting for her and wanted to be there for her, but I found myself consumed by feelings of pain and resentment. I felt abandoned all over again.

This response was quite shocking to me because until that moment, I was absolutely certain that I had let go of all those feelings of anger, resentment, and abandonment.
What made it even more shocking was I had been studying *A Course in Miracles* (ACIM) for about four years, and facilitating ACIM Study Groups for about a year. At the most basic level what ACIM teaches is *forgiveness*, though from a different perspective than the one that is conventionally held by the world.

I had overlooked this distinction and was viewing the situation from the same perspective as the *forgiveness* we practice in the world.

I Thought I Did that Already

I was so convinced that I had been practicing *Course based Forgiveness* I remained in pain, questioning whether *Course based Forgiveness* really worked, for the next three months *(can you say resistance?)* I would sit in defiance and have the following monologue:

"Forgiveness was supposed to help me be at peace regardless of what form of injustice I experienced, so why am I having a meltdown again? Maybe this only works for some types of attacks and injustices; it probably doesn't work for abandonment and emotional childhood issues like mine—especially since it happened so long ago. A Course in Miracles teaches that "Forgiveness Is the Answer"...well I already did that, but I'm still in pain and have no answers. What I'm I supposed to do now?"

I would frequently have these *Resistance Sessions*. It was not until my last one that it occurred to me, that I might not have been practicing *Course based Forgiveness* or *True Forgiveness* as the *Course* defines it. As I sat with tears streaming down my face at a total loss as to why after having forgiven my mother I was still wasn't feeling better, this thought came to mind:

"I had been practicing forgiveness since before I heard of A Course in Miracles, and even more diligently since I became a Course student, because I learned more about forgiveness from the perspective of the Course. Could I be practicing it wrong? Is this why it wasn't working for me?"

This realization came as a big relief because I felt it was very comforting to know that the problem wasn't what was taught, but my misunderstanding.

I have always looked at *Dr. Ken Wapnick* – Founder of *Foundation for A Course in Miracles*, as my Mentor. Even though I never had the opportunity to attend any of his prolific lectures, seminars classes or workshops live, I have purchased many of them over the years. I went over his material I had on hand and bought other works of his, especially those related to *forgiveness*. I also turned to *"The Circle of Atonement"* — a *Course in Miracles* oriented Teaching and Healing Center — that I have found to be invaluable in understanding the teachings of *A Course in Miracles*.

In addition to having a deep understanding and insight into ACIM and being an excellent teacher, what I found most helpful about *Ken Wapnick* was his ability to clearly articulate the *Course's* most abstract ideas and concepts in concrete and simple terms. He helped to make the *Course's* teachings practical in everyday life.

The other thing I liked was that he was always mindful of the metaphysical context within which the *Course* was written, and he emphasized the importance of that to our understanding and *living* the teachings. I found this invaluable both for my personal understanding, and in my role as a Facilitator and *Course in miracles* Teacher.

Two years after I had my *breakthrough and discovery*, I developed a workshop entitled: **Forgiveness Is the Answer**, presenting forgiveness from the perspective of *A Course in Miracles*. I offered this Workshop under that title three times a year for about four years. The content of this workshop evolved and changed as my personal understanding and healing evolved.

I later renamed it: ***True Forgiveness: the key to healing and happiness***, and developed the **5 STEP True Forgiveness Process**.

I shared this 5 Step Process with *Course in Miracles* students who were making the same mistake as I did; and in my counseling practice helping people who were struggling to let go of emotional pain. I then began offering it through *Forgiveness Coaching* to help people heal a specific issue, or as a key part of their healing and recovery program.

I would now like to share it with you because I promise you that whatever form of emotional pain you're in; or however long you've been trying to let go of it, this process will help you quickly and completely.

So, if you're open-minded, willing to consider a new perspective and ready to let go of your pain, turn the page to the next chapter and learn about the source of *True Forgiveness*.

CHAPTER II

"*A Course in Miracles*"
The Basis of *True Forgiveness*

"There's another way of looking at the world."

ACIM W-pI.33

During the mid to late nineties I was very much into self-help and personal development. Anthony Robbins was in his hay day introducing the world to what is now a household term: Life Coaching. He had launched his, Personal Power™ audio program and I had purchased a copy.

As a bonus to purchasing the Personal Power Program, you had access to a monthly two package audio series called, Power Talk. On one tape, Tony Robbins would speak on a personal development topic. The second tape would be of him interviewing a motivational speaker or another person of influence in the field of personal development.

This month in particular the guest being interviewed was sharing insights, attitudes, and perspectives in a way I had never heard from anyone else before, but at the same time sounded very familiar. It was as if I had already entertained those thoughts and ideas, and on some   level I just knew they were true.

I remember asking out loud: *Who is this guy?* That *"guy"* turned out to be *Dr. Wayne Dyer.*
In that interview *Wayne* told the story of how he had been seemingly divinely led to the grave of his father, whom he had

hated and searched for, the greater part of his adult life. *Wayne's* father was an abusive alcoholic who had left *Wayne* and his brother—both under the age of three, and their mother, and never looked back. *Wayne* and his brother had been temporarily placed in an orphanage, while their mother worked two jobs until she was able to take them back and support them.

Throughout his life, *Wayne* said he wondered how his father could have left without looking back. He said he was hoping to find his father, if for no other reason, to ask him if he had even thought to himself from time to time that he had a *"son named Wayne"*. He said he used to have dreams of meeting his father in a bar, saying: *"I'm your son, Wayne"* and literally having a, *"come to Jesus moment"* with his father.

Instead, when he got to his father's grave he broke down in tears, cried for hours, and had the most cathartic experience that he described as forgiveness. He said he felt that forgiving his father, liberating him from the judgments he had been holding against him, had also made him feel liberated himself. He said he went back home and wrote his first book, *Your Erroneous Zones*, in 18 days.

Though at the time I had no idea that I would come to see and experience *forgiveness* as an equally cathartic and transforming experience, I was deeply moved by Wayne's story. Later on in the interview when he talked about, *A Course in Miracles*, that seemed to resonate with me also. What was interesting about this was that he didn't really say very much about it.

What he said was that he had recently heard about this body of work called *"A Course in Miracles"*; that there was a lot of speculation about its origin: that it might be channeled material...about who wrote it, etc. But what he *did* know was that people who practiced its teachings claimed that they began to experience more peaceful and loving lives.

Even though the name suggested a religious text and I was not then, nor am I now "religious", something about it got my attention and seemed to call to me. It wouldn't be until a couple of years later however, after reading *Marianne Williamson's "Return To Love"* that I actually went out and bought a copy of the Second Edition of ACIM. *"Return To Love"* brought *"A Course In Miracles"* mainstream introducing many people – myself included—to the message of the *Course.*

Inspired by A Course in Miracles

The *Course's* approach to forgiveness has allowed me to let go of the fear anxiety and challenges I had been having in my attempts to practice *conventional forgiveness* i.e. *forgiveness* as it's generally defined and practiced.

Practicing *True Forgiveness* has allowed me to feel more at peace and at ease with myself, feel more worthy and valued, and experience more intimacy in my relationships because I'm no longer afraid to trust. Most importantly, practicing *True Forgiveness* as a way of life, I no longer look at anything I experience from a perspective of fear and judgment. This way I do not feel personally attacked or victimized when faced with "apparent" fearful conditions, or if I happen to be on the receiving end of the unloving words or actions of others.

I find that I'm now able to look at and respond to whatever is unfolding from a place of peace, by recognizing that it's not what happens, but the way I look at it that determines the way I experience it. This is the central lesson I have learned that has led to a more joyful, peaceful, and fulfilling experience for me in different areas of my life.

My purpose for writing this book is to share the *Course's* effective and transformative approach to *forgiveness* with those of you, who just like I used to be, are looking for a way to completely let go of some form of emotional pain or guilt; or are struggling to *forgive* yourself or another for a perceived wrongful act, or something you've experienced.

The *Course's* approach to forgiveness is empowering and practical because when practiced the effects are immediately experienced and will have a carry over effect to the next moment and/or experience. What makes this so is the *Course's metaphysically based Thought System* that is the Subject of this chapter.

My approach in writing this chapter will be to focus on the *Course's* metaphysical perspective in an attempt to bring clarity and understanding to the *Course's* teachings. As students, we very often find the *Course's* teachings inspiring and hopeful, yet, difficult to practice.

I have been teaching and facilitating ACIM study groups, classes, and workshops for 15 years and where I see people often get stuck is with the metaphysical language or terminology used in the *Course.*

Some common complaints I hear among *Course* students are: *"I know what it says, but what does it mean. I don't understand how to apply this Teaching or idea in a practical way. The Course is inspiring but not practical; or I don't know how to apply it or if it applies to my specific situation."*

I understand the feeling of frustration that I hear in the voices of my students, because I too asked the same questions during my early years as a *Course* student.

One of the reasons we find it difficult to understand what the Course is saying is because, as I mentioned earlier, the metaphysical context in which the *Course* is written. The language is metaphorical as it expresses the *Course's* abstract concepts and ideas. When the "metaphors" are taken literally you only get the surface level meaning or definition of the words, and deeper meaning remains unrecognized.

My aim is to go beyond the literal, surface level definitions of the words that are used in the *Course* and bring out the deeper underlying meaning beneath the words. This is absolutely necessary for understanding the *Course's* philosophy that is the basis of *True Forgiveness.*

That being said, this book is not intended to be a substitute for the Text of *A Course in Miracles* to learn *True Forgiveness.* If you are already a student of *A Course in Miracles*, this book can be used as a companion to facilitate your understanding and practice of *True Forgiveness.*

And, if you are not a *Course* student, but what you read in this book resonates with you in some way, or you want to learn how to live and *forgive* with ease and joy, I would encourage you to study the teachings of the *Course* for which there is no substitute.

So what is A *Course in* Miracles?

A Course in Miracles is a metaphysically based body of work that presents a radically different perspective of who we are, where we are, and what is taking place in our lives and in the world. It presents a mind re-training program to help us heal and transform our lives. Though *A Course in Miracles* usually comes under the umbrella of spirituality and is sometimes misperceived as religious, its basis is metaphysics.

Metaphysics – Practical Definition

Metaphysics is the branch of philosophy that addresses the relationship between God, man, and the universe. It attempts to answer the questions: who we are, why we're here, where we're going, and basic questions about existence and the meaning of life.

Literally defined, metaphysics is a combination of two words: the Greek word *"meta"*, meaning beyond; and *"physics"*, which is the study of the interaction between energy and matter. Put together as *"metaphysics"* that one word means: *that which lies beyond the study of the interaction between energy and matter.* In other words, the essence or the truth about what is, and what is taking place. In this case it's about how life works—so to speak—independent of your awareness, observation or beliefs.

What this means, is that the true meaning of anything does not lie in the form in which it appears but in *idea* it represents— what it really is. The word *meta* always refers to what is going on behind the scenes that causes or leads to the form that is then seen.

How It Came

The physical product that is *A Course in Miracles* is a program of spiritual psychotherapy for personal and spiritual healing and transformation. It leads us to experience more peace, happiness and fulfillment in our relationships and other areas of our lives.

The *Course* came in response to the request for *"another way"* to experience more peace in their relationship and professional lives by 2 friends and co-workers: *Bill Thetford* and *Helen Schucman*, professors and medical psychologists.

Just like we all do in similar circumstances, they had tried a variety of ways to find peace to no avail. One day one Bill said to Helen: *"There must be another way"*. Helen agreed to help him find it, and that led to the birth of the *Course*. The specific details can be found in the Preface of the Text under the Heading *"How It Came"*.

A Course in Miracles is a structured self-study program consisting of a Text with concepts, ideas, and principles that lay out the thought system; and a Workbook consisting of 365 lessons, one for each day of the year, for practical application of the principles of the Course in our daily lives. There is also a Manual for Teachers – a section written in a question and answer format, to clarify some of the central ideas presented in the Text.

What It's For

The purpose of A Course in Miracles is to provide us – as it did with Bill and Helen – with another way of looking at ourselves, our relationships and what takes place in our lives. The ultimate goal is to help us to experience more peaceful relationships, while feeling less victimized by what takes place in our lives and in the world.

A Course in Miracles teaches a new way of perceiving and interpreting what we see and experience that will allow us to entertain more empowered, peaceful, and loving thoughts about who we are; and what is taking place in every situation so we can experience our lives in this way instead.

This is what the *Course* refers to as a *"miracle"* and what it is designed to teach: how to experience love, peace, and healing regardless of circumstances or conditions that appear to be unloving, conflicting or even life threatening.

The process that leads you to experience miracles, as defined by the *Course*, is the process of letting go of the perception that will lead you to have a painful experience in some form. This process is what the Course defines as *"forgiveness"*.

The Thought System of A Course in Miracles

The *Course's* metaphysical perspective states:

- Mind is all there is
- The content of the mind is ideas
- Everything is an idea
- So everything happens in the mind

What this means for us on a practical level when it comes to our lives is that since mind is all there is:

- We have never left the mind
- What we are (we too), are ideas in the mind
- And all that is ever taking place in and as our lives is that we are experiencing the ideas in the mind in different forms.

This process can be likened to what happens during our nighttime dreams: Thoughts and ideas from our subconscious mind come into our conscious mind, appearing in symbolic forms that appear to be real.

As a matter of fact, the *Course* uses the analogy of a dream to describe our experience of being a human being – a separate individual body living in a world outside us that consists of other separate bodies and forms.

In our nighttime dreams, because we are not aware that we are dreaming and think the symbolic forms are real, we respond to them emotionally, physiologically, and physically. We may cry, break into a sweat, or even physically strike out if we are dreaming of being attacked.

When we awake however, we feel safe and at peace realizing that we were never really threatened or in danger, because we never left the confines of our bed.

The *Course* describes our perception of our life in the world as, dreaming a dream of separation. The teachings of the *Course* are like "little nudges" coming from outside the dream to help us realize that we're dreaming. The "miracle" the *Course* is designed to teach, is the realization, that you're dreaming a dream of separation, and the dream you're dreaming is false.

In the following section I would like to share 12 central lessons that teach the metaphysical facts or "Truth" about who we are, where we are, and what is taking place in our lives and the world.

12 CENTRAL LESSONS

LESSON #1
THERE'S ANOTHER WAY OF LOOKING AT THE WORLD
(W-pI.33)

This lesson is the foundation for understanding the metaphysical thought system of *A Course in Miracles*. It is like a directive or a compass pointing you towards the direction in which you need to go, for healing and transforming your life —your mind.

Essentially, it's teaching that you don't have to change circumstances or conditions in order to change a painful experience. You can change your experience by changing the way you are looking at the circumstance or condition, that you perceive to be causing you pain.

This lesson is not teaching you to think positive, rationalize, or deny what you are seeing and feeling. It's the underlying metaphysical truth that is the reason we experience anything the way we do. It is not because of *what* happens, but because of the way we look at it.

Be aware that the word *"world"*, as it is used in this context, is not limited to planet earth or the world at large, but is used as a metaphor for whatever happens to be the object of your attention in any given moment; and/or to the situation or condition that is the focus of your attention.

What this lesson teaches is that everything happens in the mind.

What this means for you on a personal level is that the nature of an experience, situation, or condition does not determine how you will feel, how you will be affected, or how you should respond to it. If and/or how you're affected by anything you experience or encounter is based solely on the way you look at it: your perception, what you believe to be true?

The next lesson defines what determines your perception.

LESSON #2
I AM NEVER UPSET FOR THE REASON I THINK
(W-pI.5)

This lesson makes us aware of the fact that we don't know or understand the true cause of our sadness, anger, pain, or fear. We need to change our perception to see another way of viewing the world. This lays the groundwork for *True Forgiveness*.

We firmly believe that the reason we get upset, angry or afraid is because of something we have experienced or encountered, or because of something that has happened in the world.

This lesson teaches otherwise. Stemming from the content in the text, this lesson suggests that the *only* reason we get worked up is because we have chosen to accept the ego's thought system, or perspective from which to look at and interpret the world.

The ego's thought system says: "You're a separate body; living in a world outside; to which you are *subject* or a *victim*."

According to the ego, the world is real. The *Course* teaches there are only two thought systems or perspectives through which we can view the world. The ego is one and the other is what the *Course* calls the Holy Spirit's perspective, or the perspective of Truth.

We can only choose one of these two perspectives to be true for us because they each contain directly opposing ideas. Choosing one automatically closes or blocks off your awareness of the other, and you will see and experience the world from the perspective that you have chosen.

In choosing the ego's perspective, we believe the pain, problems, and fear we experience in the world has a physical cause, but the truth is, all problems are problems of perception, or rather, misperceptions based on misunderstanding or lack of awareness of the truth.

LESSON #3
I AM NOT THE VICTIM OF THE WORLD I SEE
(W-pI.31)

The idea taught in this lesson is like the sledgehammer or wrecking ball. It knocks down the supporting structure for the ego fear-based, perspective that we hold onto.

The ego's perspective leads us to see ourselves as products of our environment. We believe that what we do, the experiences we have, and the conditions to which we're subjected – especially during our childhood or formative years – mold and shape who we become; and can direct or determine the path and quality of our adult life.

This is the reason why people who were either born into or experienced dire or challenging circumstances early in life, and thrived, are said to have beaten the odds. This is based on the misperception that we are victims of circumstance.

The title of this lesson clearly states this is not the case and the body of this lesson opens with the following words: *"Today's idea is the introduction to your declaration of release."* (W-pI.31.1:1)

The rest of the lesson reinforces the idea that perceiving the situations and experiences that we have as being the determiner of who we become, and the director of our paths, is a lie stemming from misunderstanding and misperception.

Everything is a reflection or projection of an idea in the mind. Ideas cannot attack, make, or cause anything to happen.

LESSON #4
FEAR IS NEVER JUSTIFIED IN ANY FORM
(W-pII.240)

This lesson implies that everything we experience in any form is fear. Perception of "fear" is the cause of our experiencing pain and problems. The idea of *forgiveness* is the realization that the only thing we're up against in the world is in our mind.

"Fear" in this sense is the idea behind the acronym: False Evidence Appearing Real: what we see and believe when we accept the ego's perspective of the world and everything that takes place in it as real.

Nothing we see or experience in any form has substance, power, or meaning in and of itself. Anything in any form that appears fearful or threatening is literally *nothing but a bad idea*.

Bad ideas are not to be taken seriously. How you respond to them is to simply let them go.

LESSON #5
I AM NOT A BODY. I AM FREE.
(W-pI.199)

This lesson is a major theme and a central idea of the *Course's* thought system or perspective. Identifying ourselves with our bodies is what keeps us from letting go of the ego's thought system. It keeps us tied to pain and problems and the belief that we are victims of the world.

When we feel vulnerable or threatened, it is only because we think we are a body. As long as we believe we are a body we will experience pain in some form. It is essentially our *belief that we are a body* that is experienced in different forms of pain.

The truth is that we are an idea, and remain unaffected and unchanged.

This lesson dispels the thought or misperception of yourself as a body, by pointing your attention to the truth that you are an idea in the mind: unbounded, invulnerable, and free.

The metaphysical idea being presented here is that all disease, discontent, or experiences of lack or limitation, are nothing other than the effect of perceiving yourself other than what you really are.

LESSON #6
TRUTH WILL CORRECT ALL THE ERRORS IN MY MIND
(W-pI.107)

This lesson is an implicit reminder that it is the errors in thinking that need to be corrected for peace and healing to occur.

Like the previous lesson, we're being taught that misperceiving ourselves as bodies, leads us to feeling fearful, vulnerable and constantly under threat.

This lesson teaches that choosing the thought system or perspective of Truth, will correct those errors in thinking that lead to misperceptions in which we identify ourselves falsely.

Nothing ever happens *to* you, rather everything happens *through* you—through the thoughts you entertain and accept to be the truth, and the interpretations and judgments that you make as a result.

LESSON #7
ALL THINGS ARE LESSONS GOD WOULD HAVE ME LEARN
(W-pI.193)

This lesson teaches three central *Course* themes or ideas:

1. We are here to learn
2. What we teach, we learn
3. *Forgiveness* is what we are here to learn

In the *Course*, God, truth, and love are one and the same. The *Course* teaches that only love is real/truth, love is all there is, God is love, and the opposite of love is fear.

Fear is of the idea of believing that the world is real, and leads us to attack, as well as judge and place conditions upon the world. Love, being its opposite, must be the idea that sees the world as unreal, and leads us to allow, accept, include, and let all things be, without judgment or conditions.

If love and God are one, and only love/God is real then love/God is All there is. The *Course* describes the "world" as a classroom, for learning or re-learning the truth that only love/God is real.

We learn this by looking at every moment, relationship, or experience in the world in which we are not at peace as opportunities to remind us that it is not real, and in so doing re-learn the Truth.

We need to be willing to recognize that each fearful or threatening feeling or experience is a *lesson*, teaching us that we have placed a metaphorical block to our awareness of and the experience of love/truth the only thing that is real.

LESSON #8
I LOOSE THE WORLD FROM ALL I THOUGHT IT WAS
(W-pI.132)

This lesson is re-directing our awareness towards our minds so we can recognize and experience the truth, and away from the ego and the false evidence appearing as Truth or real in different forms of the outside world.

We put a lot of faith in the physical world —what we encounter through our senses. We have given it a lot of power and we judge everything in the world according to appearances. The *Course* describes it as a hierarchy of illusions because nothing here is real. It is all, illusory. We believe some things are better, have more value, and can make us happier, safer, more worthy etc.

As long as we look to the world for guidance, love, safety or truth we'll be going down the wrong path because we will have once again accepted the ego's lie. We will take issue with what appears to be attacks and threats, and try to defend against them, feeling the need to change or fix something outside us to experience the truth.

The Voice of truth says that experiencing peace, safety, or healing in any area of your life rests solely on changing your perception and not situation, circumstance, or condition.

LESSON #9
I COULD SEE PEACE INSTEAD OF THIS
(W-pI.34)

Our perception determines the way we see and experience what takes place in the world and in our lives.

This lesson leaves no room for doubt or question and it's not open for discussion. It is a statement that suggests peace is a choice. The *Course* teaches that every choice is a choice for peace, or nothing.

What this means, is that peace comes as a result of *choosing peace*, and not from choosing something that you think will bring you peace. This is because everything that you see here in any form is nothing but the reflection of an idea in the mind.

You know you have chosen nothing by the lack of peace you're experiencing in any moment or situation; and how you choose peace is by being willing to experience peace instead.

LESSON #10
JUDGMENT AND LOVE ARE OPPOSITES
(W-pII.352)

This lesson is specifically about what will hinder your practice of *forgiveness* or make *forgiving* seem painful.

Judgment is another form in which fear is experienced and expressed. Judgment is looking at the world and what takes place in it as real and having the power to affect us; or looking at actions or behavior as sinful, wrong, and requiring punishment.

Remember that love is to accept, allow, include, and let all things be without judgment or conditions.

You cannot entertain two opposing or conflicting thoughts, and you cannot entertain one thought and expect to experience effects that are not reflective of that thought.

If you are entertaining thoughts of judgment to any degree, or in any form, you will not be able to look at anything from a perspective of love i.e. from the perspective that will allow you to see nothing as an attack or in need of pardoning. This is what makes *forgiving* or letting go possible.

As long as you are entertaining thoughts of judgment, *forgiving* will feel unfair and more like a sacrifice that inflicts pain. *True Forgiveness* at its core, is simply recognizing the illusory nature of the form in which anything appears. So, you realize it's *nothing*, and being nothing has done nothing to you in any way.

LESSON #11
I AM ENTITLED TO MIRACLES
(W-pI.77)

This lesson teaches us what a miracle is and how to experience one. We are *entitled* to miracles, and we learn in the body of the lesson that we cannot receive miracles without giving miracles.

From the perspective of the world a miracle is something given to us by or from God, and it usually involves some physical or bodily change.

From the perspective of the *Course*, a miracle is a change in the *perception* of a physical or bodily condition, and may or may not include actual changes in any form.

Being free and having the right to change our perception regarding any situation or condition is what it means to be *entitled* to miracles. In having the *right* to change our perception, we have the *right* to experience miracles.

To give or extend a miracle is to look at something or someone from the perspective of, or through, eyes of love. Again, this requires that we let go of our fear-based perception of that other person or thing. In shifting from our fear-based perception, we experience it in the form of love. That's the miracle. It's the experience of love, and as we experience love, that's what we give.

Both giving and receiving miracles are the same, so you must give miracles in order to receive miracles.

LESSON #12
FORGIVENESS ENDS THE DREAM OF CONFLICT HERE
(W-pII.333)

This is a lesson in *True Forgiveness.*

When you forgive from the perspective of the *Course,* what you are forgiving or letting go of is "an idea"—the idea that something was really done to you by another that has caused you some form of harm, loss, or pain.

Forgiving in this way rests on the *Course's* most fundamental teaching: *"It's not what happens, but the way you look at it, that determines the way you experience it".* This is recognizing and acknowledging that everything happens in the mind and that you're never threatened or in danger from anything or anyone in the world.

This form of *Forgiveness – True forgiveness* is the other way the *Course* is teaching us to experience lasting peace, healing, and a feeling of safety, while living in a world that seems to threaten us at every turn.

True forgiveness, seeing past the seeming reality or the myriad illusory forms we constantly come up against and recognizing them as *nothing but* illusory forms, is the only way we will let go of those painful experiences without fear or feeling further victimized.

The truth is you will always and only experience the content of your thoughts in its exact nature, in some form. *True Forgiveness* is recognizing this so you don't fall into *"the temptation to perceive yourself unfairly treated."* (T-26.X.4:1)

I have chosen the 12 lessons above because they reflect the central underlying themes – or heartbeat - of *Course Based Forgiveness* or *True Forgiveness*.

The following Chapter looks at why *Conventional Forgiveness*, unlike *Course based forgiveness*, generates fear, is difficult to practice and because of the way it's defined, keeps you in pain.

SECTION II

UNDERSTANDING

TRUE FORGIVENESS

CHAPTER III

Why You Struggle with *Forgiveness*

"Forgiveness is not what you think"

Don't Talk to *Me* about Forgiveness

I had offered the original Forgiveness Workshop under the title of: ***"Forgiveness Is the Answer"*** about three times a year from 2005-2008. During that time, the content of the workshop evolved as my own understanding and practice of the *Course's* perspective of *forgiveness* evolved. Each time I presented the workshop, the content was presented a little differently to lend clarity and understanding.

I experienced my biggest breakthrough during the early part of 2009, so as I was preparing for the Spring 2009 workshop, I had the feeling of completion. I felt that except for changing or adding certain stories, or examples to illustrate an idea or support my teaching, there was nothing else I needed to add or change to make the metaphysical perspective of *forgiveness*, more understandable.

During the years I had been facilitating this workshop, a common experience among participants was that the ideas sounded doable in theory, but were difficult to apply in practice. This was not because they were complicated, but because the *Course's* perspective of *forgiveness* stems from metaphysics. Just like the teachings of the Course, the terminology and perspective is metaphorical and abstract, so like students of *A Course in Miracles*, Workshop participants found the approach to *forgiveness* inspiring, but difficult to apply.

One of the first major changes I made to the Workshop – in addition to the **5 Step Process** - was to add a list of clarifications of some of the key metaphorical terms, used in relation to *forgiveness*. (See Appendix at the back of this book).

This made a significant difference both in helping me to better explain the concept of *True Forgiveness* to my workshop participants; and to help them understand how to apply what they were learning to get their desired results.

The next change was the title from: *"**Forgiveness Is the Answer**"* to *"**True Forgiveness: the Key to Healing and Happiness**"*. In the Spring of 2009 (with permission from the participants, of course) I recorded my first **True Forgiveness Workshop**. I turned that recording into a CD Set that was given to each of the Participants as part of the Materials Package.

One day shortly after the Workshop I had a copy of it in my car that I was listening to on my way to pick up a friend for lunch. As she settled into the seat she noticed the CD Case, picked it up and asked: *"What's this?"* I told her what it was and without missing a beat she said: *"Forgiveness...don't talk to me about forgiveness..."*

In a voice filled with emotion she related the details of a situation with a family member, who had behaved in a manner that was nothing short of a betrayal.

She described how deeply wounded she had been feeling; and how the family member had shown neither concern nor remorse. How could she be expected to *"forgive that?"*

As I listened to my friend, I understood exactly where she was coming from. She was feeling, fearing, and anticipating some or all of the following, as we all do when we attempt to practice conventional forgiveness:

- You're willing to forgive but you're afraid you might get hurt again
- You want to forgive but forgiving feels like you're letting the wrongdoer get away with something or without paying in some way for their wrongful act
- You secretly, or not so secretly, think that forgiveness = weakness
- You think you've forgiven something, yet you're still triggered by and find yourself forgiving the same thing repeatedly and continue to experience resentment
- Maybe you just can't or don't want to forgive because you think what was done in your case was unforgiveable
- Perhaps you think the wrongdoer is undeserving of forgiveness
- Or maybe you would forgive, but you don't know how

The Real Problem with Conventional Forgiveness

Merriam-Webster defines forgiveness as: to stop feeling anger toward (someone who has done something wrong): *to stop blaming (someone); to stop feeling anger about (something): to forgive someone for (something wrong: to stop requiring payment of (money that is owed)*

Some synonyms for forgiveness are: pardon – absolution – mercy – exoneration – dispensation as in waiving or dismissing the wrongful act or payment.

This definition of *forgiveness* and what it suggests that you need to do in order to *forgive* is the #1 reason why we struggle with *forgiveness*. They stem from certain misperceptions about forgiveness that make the idea of forgiving seem unfair and the practice of forgiveness feel painful.

Also, when you closely examine this definition what you're being asked to do that is described as *forgiving* can really only be done as a **result** of having *forgiven*.

The following are five of the most common misperceptions that lead to struggle in our practice.

MISPERCEPTION #1: Forgiveness is Something that Takes Place Between People

A generally accepted belief of *Conventional Forgiveness*, is that it is something that is done to someone or by someone: whether it's God granting *forgiveness* to a repentant sinner through the priest, or a person who has been wronged granting *forgiveness* to the wrongdoer. *Forgiveness*, from the perspective of the world, is something that must be given to or from another.

This requires that the person who has been wronged, must be willing to grant *forgiveness*, to the person who has wronged them. This however, will pose a problem if the person who feels they have been wronged is not willing to grant *forgiveness* to the wrongdoer.

MISPERCEPTION #2: Forgiveness Must Be Earned or Deserving

This misperception follows along the same vein as the first, which is, since forgiveness must be granted to the wrongdoer by the wronged, the wrongdoer must show remorse, or apologize for their wrongdoing in order for it to be granted.

The thinking as a result of this misperception is that the person who has been wronged needs an apology from the wrongdoer and/or show some kind of remorse to prove their deservedness. In the case where the wrongdoer refuses to apologize or show remorse, the person who has been wronged will feel that *forgiveness* is undeserving.

MISPERCEPTION #3: Forgiving You Means Speaking to You

I once walked away from a social relationship with someone after I realized it was neither a loving nor peaceful experience for either of us. I felt no animosity towards this person. I just became aware that this relationship was built on fear because interacting with them was not a peaceful experience. So, choosing peace, I walked away.

I had not spoken to this person for a few years when a mutual friend of ours called, saying that "our mutual friend" had shared with her that they had not been feeling very peaceful about the way our friendship had ended, and wanted us to be on speaking terms again, so they could find peace.

I shared with her, that not speaking to our mutual friend did not mean I considered them my enemy; nor did being on speaking terms with them mean that we were friends.

My friend responded somewhat accusingly: *"What about forgiveness Jenn. I know how you feel about forgiveness."*

I shared that because we looked at forgiveness differently, I had actually practiced *forgiveness* in its truest sense, by recognizing the true cause of my lack of peace in the relationship with our mutual friend and addressing the cause rather than blaming them.

You don't need to speak to someone to *forgive. Forgiveness* is a process that takes place in your mind.

MISPERCEPTION #4: To Forgive You Must Let Go of the Desire to Punish or Condemn

This misperception makes *forgiveness* difficult and painful to practice, because it suggests that you are acknowledging that there **is** a call for punishment or condemnation, but **you should not want** to execute it.

If you perceive something as an act of wrongdoing or as a sin, you are saying that something real has occurred; and punishment will always be seen as the justifiable response.

It will therefore seem unfair not to want to respond in a manner that you think is just, and it will be painful if you don't because it will feel like justice has not been served.

MISPERCEPTION #5: Some Things Are More Difficult to Forgive than Others and Some Things Are Unforgiveable

This misperception rests on our belief that the words and actions of others and the things that happen to us affect us. Some things are seen as worse than others. For example, we believe that physical blows will affect us more severely than being spoken to in harsh words. Loss of property is not as bad as the loss of a body part.

Naturally, we will not only find it more difficult to *forgive* certain acts, or persons based on the severity of their actions, but if seen as extremely severe, we'll find it impossible to *forgive* at all.

Also, the nature of the act, and whether it was accidental or done deliberately, along with the perpetrator's story, all comes into play from this *misperception*. We will find it easier to consider *forgiving* an accidental misdeed, but not a deliberate act of cruelty. We can forgive an act of cruelty expressed by someone who may have suffered acts of cruelty themselves, based on the assumption that they may not know any other way. However, if this person is deliberately cruel, and on top of that we learn that they've had a perfect pain-free life well...that would be *unforgiveable*.

The Source of these MISPERCEPTIONS

The *Course* teaches, *"Projection makes Perception."* This means that we have certain ideas in our mind about what is true. These ideas determine the way we will see and experience everything that happens in our lives and in the world. So the content of these ideas then is *projected*, like images in a mirror, onto everything we see and experience determining what anything will mean to us.

Since projection makes perception, when you hold a perspective of victimization you cannot not see the world, and what you experience in it as real and having real effects on you in some way. It is this misunderstanding, and misperceiving the illusory nature of what happens in the world as real, that leads to the **misperceptions** about *forgiveness* that causes us to struggle with it.

The *Course* describes the nature of the struggle this way:

> **"How can you overlook what you have made real? By seeing it clearly, you have made it real and cannot overlook it."** (T-9.IV.4:5)

The problem with *forgiveness* is the misperception of:

- Who we are
- Where we are
- What is taking place
- How to respond to what's taking place
- And, why respond in that way

Let me share what I mean: I called to invite a friend to attend the first workshop I was facilitating under the new Title of ***"True Forgiveness."*** She had attended a few of my lectures in the past, as she said she always enjoyed and felt inspired by the metaphysical perspective I shared in my message.

She thanked me for inviting her but declined the invitation because she said she *"didn't have anything to forgive"*. She wished me luck, and then asked, almost as an after thought: *"Why do you call it True Forgiveness anyway?"*

I told her it was a perspective of *Forgiveness* based on the same metaphysical perspective that I always speak and teach about; that she has shared she finds inspiring, and that, as a matter of fact, was what made me think of inviting her.

I shared that what led me to develop the workshop in the first place, was because of the breakthrough I had in 2004 about what *forgiveness* really is, and what it means to *forgive*. I shared further that understanding and practicing this form of *forgiveness* over the years has allowed me to let go of the feelings of fear and resentment that often accompanied my attempts at *forgiveness*. I told her that for me, this form of *forgiveness* is a way of living that is allowing me to feel less victimized, by those circumstances or conditions that can sometimes seem so threatening.

I shared that it is called *True Forgiveness* because, when this form of *forgiveness* is practiced, it always leads us to experience the peace, joy and healing that we struggle to experience practicing *Conventional Forgiveness.*

Who Is True Forgiveness for?

If you are in any of the following situations and what you are doing to get your desired results is not working; or you don't know what to do to find the peace or healing that you seek than *True Forgiveness* will help you:

- You're practicing forgiveness as a form of spiritual practice, but you're struggling.
- You're in a recovery program and forgiving is essential to your healing, but you're finding it more painful than healing.
- You've experienced some form of attack or abuse and can't seem to move forward. You can't let go of the pain or painful thoughts about the experience.
- You have experienced some form of betrayal in a relationship and are having difficulty rebuilding trust, or you have agreed to let it go, but can't seem to forget it.
- You are plagued by guilt over some things you might have done or said for which you judge yourself.
- You have unresolved painful childhood issues that still seem to cause you pain and/or affect the choices that you make.
- You're harboring thoughts of regret and blame about your lot in life and missed opportunities.
- You secretly feel unworthy and entertain thoughts of shame.

Ending the Struggle

True Forgiveness will allow you to find the peace and healing you are seeking if you are experiencing any of the above situations. The reason you experience any of the above is the same reason why you struggle with *conventional forgiveness*: Entertaining a misperception of what is the true cause of your pain or discontent, and what to do about it.

Whether it's looked at from the perspective of the world or the perspective of *A Course In Miracles, "Forgiveness"* is about *"letting go"* of something that is causing you to experience a lack of peace, discontent or some form of pain.

True Forgiveness is changing your perception of what it is you're letting go of, so that the idea of *forgiving* doesn't seem unfair, and the process of forgiving as fearless, simple and pain-free.

In the next Chapter, you're going to learn what it is that makes *"True Forgiveness"* the metaphorical "key" to healing and happiness.

CHAPTER IV

The *"Dynamics"* of *True Forgiveness*

"Forgiveness is your function"
A Course in Miracles

This Chapter will focus on the *Course in Miracles'* philosophy of *forgiveness* and why it should matter to you. We'll be looking at:

- The *Course's* perspective of *forgiveness*
- Why you should practice *Course based forgiveness*
- How *Course based forgiveness* differs from *conventional forgiveness*

The *Course's* Perspective of *Forgiveness*

I fondly refer to my husband as, *Honest Abe* because among the many loving ways he shows up in life, he is honest to a fault. One night I had a dream that he and I were in the car on our way home from somewhere and because of a detour, we found ourselves walking along what looked like railroad tracks beneath the highway.

We come upon a man's briefcase.

My husband suggested that I look inside to see if there was any ID while he checked the surroundings for any other related items. In the briefcase I found a billfold with ID and huge wad of cash. I want to keep the cash, but I know if I show the billfold with the ID to my husband, he'll never let me. If I took out the cash and just gave him the billfold, when we contacted the owner they would know that I stolen their money.

So I take the cash, toss the billfold away, and tell *Honest Abe* I didn't find any ID in the briefcase, and then we're back in the car heading home. As we drove, I started having this immense feeling of guilt over what I'd done because it was so out of character. When I woke up, I felt horrible until I realized it was just a dream—I had done nothing—so there was nothing to feel guilty about. I had an immense feeling of relief and joy at the realization that it was only a dream.

I share this story because *A Course in Miracles* uses the analogy of a dream to describe our experience of being in individual human bodies, living in a world outside of us. Things happen that aren't always logical. In daily life, we do and say things and behave in ways that are not at all characteristic of who we are, or that are kind, honest and loving.

We all know this immense feeling of guilt.

From the perspective of *A Course in Miracles*, this is the only thing that is taking place in our experiences from birth to death; and regardless of how many lifetimes we think we've lived—it's all a dream.

In Chapter 10, Section I, **At Home in God**, the *Course* describes what is taking place in this way:

"You're at home in God, dreaming of exile but perfectly capable of awakening to reality. Is it your decision to do so? You recognize from your own experience that what you see in dreams is real while you are asleep. Yet the instant you awaken you realize that everything that seemed to happen in the dream did not happen at all. You do not think this strange, even though all the laws to what you awaken to were violated while you slept. Is it not possible that you

merely shifted from one dream to another, without really waking?" **(T-10.I.2.1-6)**

This analogy of 'the world as a dream' is what the *Course* means by the idea that everything happens in the mind. It doesn't *deny* that you're experiencing the things you do it means they're not taking place where you think – not in a world outside you.

There is a lot of mystery and misperception surrounding dreams. Some people see dreams as prophetic, providing insight and guidance if properly understood. Others believe that our dreams are about real experiences that take place in another realm or plane of existence.

The truth is, that dreams are the ideas from our subconscious mind, coming into our awareness, because the conscious part of our mind is completely relaxed while we are asleep. So those thoughts that are usually held in check, freely float into our awareness showing up in symbolic forms.

In our dreams – we go nowhere, we do nothing, and nothing really happens. The images, objects, and places that we see are not real. They are all illusory - symbolic projections of thoughts and ideas from within our subconscious mind.

What the Idea that You Are Dreaming Has To Do with *Forgiveness*

If our experience of living in a world of suffering and pain is a dream, we will continue to see it, experience it, and respond to it as if it is real, until we wake from the dream and realize we are dreaming.

Looking at our experience of life in the world as nothing but a dream, is what will allow us to let go of the belief that anything **is** the cause of our feelings, or **can** cause us pain or suffering.

This, from the perspective of the *Course*, is what *True Forgiveness* is because you'll be recognizing and letting go of the true cause of your pain.

Why Practice *Course Based Forgiveness*

A Course in Miracles teaches that *Forgiveness* is our function and that our happiness and our function are one. What this means for us with regards to living in the world, is that we are to *forgive* as a way of life i.e. *forgiveness* should be our *only* response, regardless of what we experience. *Forgiving* is what will make us happy, which is how we should be, regardless of what we experience in our lives.

The true source of pain in any experience is not what is said or done, or happens, but the fear that it could negatively affect your life in some way. You will continue to respond this way and be unhappy as long as you continue to see the physical world as real.

The *Course* sees **guilt** as stemming from our misperception of the world and the things we do. This is because we will always and only experience the content of our thoughts and beliefs. *Guilt* in the context within which the *Course* is speaking is, "the belief that a **G**odless – **U**njust – **I**nsane – **L**acking – **T**ragic thought is real"

The world, as it appears, is a mirror image reflection of the above definition of guilt:

- As a general rule we feel God is absent from the world and we need to do certain things such as pray to bring the presence and power of God into the world or in our lives.
- Life certainly seems unfair and unjust. The things that go on in the world sometimes seem quite mad or at least, illogical.

- We always seem to be lacking something.
- In addition to this, everything ends in some form of loss or tragedy: first, regardless of how well someone lives, how much they contribute or make the world a better place, they eventually die. All relationships come to an end, everything ceases to "be" at some point and loss and sadness is felt as a result.
- So-called natural disasters are constantly taking place in the world and always have tragic consequences.

A couple of years ago I found myself in a situation by which I was feeling extremely victimized. The specific circumstances and people involved aren't important, because the specifics of any situation are never what matters. From the *Course's* perspective: it's not what happens, but the way you look at it that determines the way you experience it.

The way you look at anything and what **does** matter—the **only** thing that matters in any situation or circumstance—is the inner conversation you're having about what the situation means; if and how it's affecting you; and what, or if anything you believe has to change or happen, in order for you to feel safe, happy or at peace.

My inner conversation during this situation was about how I was being treated in very unloving ways. I was telling myself that the way I was being treated meant neither I, nor my feelings mattered. I had an inner dialogue of, *"I am alone, unloved, unsupported, and very wounded"*. I was telling myself I needed emotional support from others—especially those close to me—in order for me to feel loved, and emotionally equipped to survive the situation.

Even though I had been using *Course based Forgiveness/True Forgiveness* in my coaching and counseling Practice and facilitating *True Forgiveness Workshops*; I have to admit I was not yet practicing *True Forgiveness* exclusively in my own life. Occasionally, I would resort to what I call the, *"Attitudinal*

A.D.D approach of Conventional Forgiveness," in which, what you do in an attempt to forgive is: *"Avoid thinking about the person or situation that is causing you pain and deny that you are feeling victimized, upset, or troubled by it".* If you can do neither of those things, or if you're still troubled, *"distract yourself in some way to avoid feeling the pain".*

Of course, this does not work and did not work for me. During that period I became increasingly stressed, almost to the point of an emotional breakdown. When I became willing to look at the situation differently, I realized that this situation was not here to hurt me. It was an opportunity to help me.

I chose to look at the situation through the eyes of *Forgiveness* instead of fear and judgment. It was at this point I began to practice *True Forgiveness* exclusively, applying the 5 STEP FORGIVENESS PROCESS to heal my painful situation.

By practicing *True Forgiveness* I was able to completely let go of feeling victimized by that situation, without needing to change it in any way. What I learned was that this seemingly painful situation, was the necessary classroom for me to learn and master the practice of *True Forgiveness.*

This experience was the catalyst for writing this book. It allowed me to understand in a deeply personal way, what it means, that it's not what happens but how you look at it, that determines the way you experience it.

When I looked at my situation as something coming to help me and not to hurt me, I saw it as the opportunity to help me do what it is I'm here to do: master the practice of *True Forgiveness* and share it with others like you. When you become willing to look at all things through the eyes of *Forgiveness*, instead of fear and judgment, you will see that nothing comes to hurt you; rather everything serves the purpose of your healing and awakening.

How *Course Based Forgiveness* Differs from *Conventional Forgiveness*

The following cartoon illustrates the world's perspective of *forgiveness* as something that takes place between people and sees words, actions, and behavior as being necessary for the process:

"Do you have a card that stops short of saying 'I'm sorry' yet vaguely hints of some wrongdoing?"

The *Course's* perspective of *forgiveness* is quite different as it rests on the perception of the world as the reflection of an idea. What you're *forgiving*, i.e. letting go of, in any situation is not something that was said or done, or some feeling that you have as a result of something that was said or done. All you're *forgiving, letting go of*, in every instance is *"an idea"*.

What Course based forgiveness is not:
  ▪ It is not about rationalizing the actions or behavior of another so you don't feel hurt by what they do or say

- It is not about putting a positive spin on something to justify it so you don't feel bad about it or victimized
- It's not about denying or ignoring what you're feeling or thinking about the thing that's causing you pain

The *Course's* Basis of *True Forgiveness*

In the Workbook of *A Course In Miracles*, the first paragraph of the answer to the question: *"What Is Forgiveness?"* addresses the basis of *True Forgiveness*. The paragraph reads:

"Forgiveness recognizes that what you thought your brother did to you has not occurred. It does not pardon sins and make them real. It sees there was no sin. And in that view, are all your sins forgiven. What is sin, except a false idea about God's Son? Forgiveness merely sees its falsity, and therefore lets it go. What then is free to take its place is now the Will of God." **(W-pII.1.1:1-7)**

This paragraph, in essence, echoes the *Course's* perspective of the world as a dream, and everything that takes place in it is *an illusion*. This idea is the basis of *forgiving* as the *Course* teaches.

As *A Course in Miracles* says with regards to learning and accepting anything it teaches, all that's required to accept the perception of the world as an illusion, so you don't feel victimized in any situation, is *"a little willingness"*.

This basically means just being *willing to consider* that what the *Course* is teaching is true, and to begin to question the validity of what you have been accepting without question, to be the truth.

If you're having difficulty even considering this perspective, consider the words in the passage I shared at the beginning of this Chapter, from Chapter 10 of the Text of *A Course in*

Miracles that in essence, tells us: We're dreaming a dream *"but perfectly capable of awakening to reality."* (W-10.2.1). In addition, the *Course* suggests that awakening to reality is *"our decision"*.

Practicing *Course based forgiveness* is the way we make the *decision* to awaken to reality. Awakening to reality simply means recognizing the illusory nature of everything you see or encounter, in any form of pain or conflict in the world. Since the *Course* teaches that *forgiveness is our function*, and that happiness and our function are one, this suggests that *forgiveness* as the *Course* teaches it, is the way we are to be, operate and respond to everything and everyone, as a way of life.

In doing so we let go of feeling betrayed, attacked, hurt, unfairly treated or victimized by a world outside. We perform our *function* and as a result feel empowered, happy, and at peace regardless of circumstances, situations, or conditions.

So if you are struggling with your practice of *forgiveness*, or are often troubled by some form of emotional pain— betrayal—guilt—feelings of unworthiness etc.—to borrow a line from the *Course*: ***"This Need Not Be."*** (T-4.IV.h)

Forgiveness—True Forgiveness, is the key to healing and happiness and in the next Chapter you will learn the #1 Requirement for practicing *True Forgiveness,* to bring about the lasting healing and happiness that you seek.

CHAPTER V

Developing the

Consciousness for True Forgiveness

"All things are lessons God would have me learn."
ACIM W-pI.193

It is said that if you start with the wrong premise, regardless of how logical your arguments, you'll never arrive at the right conclusion. The world, in which *Conventional Forgiveness* is seen as valid, started with the wrong premise.

This premise holds that the world and everything in it is real, unpredictable, and not safe. In short, you see yourself as a *victim* of the world.

This gives rise to a *consciousness of victimization*. By this I don't mean not being able to get past or overcome some circumstance, challenge, or condition, but believing there's a *"cause-and-effect"* relationship between the circumstances, challenges, and conditions you encounter in the world, and what you feel.

It is this premise that gives rise to the consciousness for *Conventional Forgiveness*, and the difficulty we run into as we try to practice *forgiveness* the way we do in the world.

Albert Einstein said: *"Problems cannot be solved with the same mind that created them."* True forgiveness cannot be practiced from a consciousness that stems from a *consciousness of victimization*. In order to completely let go of feeling victimized by what you experience in the world, and let go of the fear of the possibility of being hurt or unfairly treated in any way, you **must** develop the **Consciousness for True Forgiveness**.

Consciousness consists of the beliefs/premises, attitudes, interpretations you make, thoughts you think, and your responses regarding five metaphysical facts:
- Who you are
- Where you are
- What is taking place
- How to respond to what is taking place
- Why respond in that way

This chapter will focus on the # 1 Requirement for practicing *True Forgiveness*. That is: entertaining the mindset for the *Consciousness for True Forgiveness*. This will allow you to recognize and acknowledge the Truth about the first three above-mentioned metaphysical facts because misperceiving these three is the equivalent of starting with the wrong *premise*.

This Chapter will look at:
- The Right Mindset – set of beliefs
- How to develop and maintain the Right Mindset
- The true perspective of *Forgiveness*
- The foundation and the facts of *True Forgiveness*

After reading this chapter you will learn the truth about the Right Mindset – and it's not *"Positive Thinking"*. You will know how to develop and maintain the consciousness for practicing *True Forgiveness*, and you will learn the three major blocks that can sabotage your consciousness for *True Forgiveness*, and how to recognize and release them.

Defining Mindset

The first step in developing the *Consciousness for Forgiveness* is considering another way of looking at who you are, where you are, and what is taking place, in and as your life and in the world – *Entertain the right mindset.*

Your mindset is not just the thoughts in your mind at any given moment or what you may be thinking about a particular subject, object, or person. Your "mindset" consists of your underlying paradigm — the framework of ideas you hold about what life is and how life works.

The following diagram that I've borrowed and adapted from my mentor *Dr. Ken Wapnick*, provides a graphic illustration of this process:

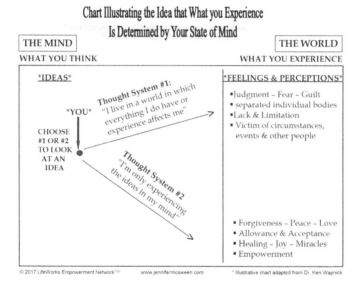

Resting on the *Course's* perspective that everything happens in the mind, this illustration shows that we can only choose from one of two thought systems from which to look at the world. Thought System #1 (ego's thought system) gives rise to a mindset of victimization. You look at the world as real and you think of, and experience it from a perspective of fear, pain, and judgment.

Thought System #2 (Holy Spirit's, or the thought system of Truth) will allow you to hold an empowering mindset. You will look at the world as the *Course* sees it: a reflection or "witness to your state of mind". You will think of and experience everything that takes place in the world from a perspective of peace and without fear or judgment, i.e. from a perspective of love. This is the correct thought system to use, and the right mindset to entertain.

Entertaining the Right Mindset

The Right Mindset for developing the *Consciousness for True Forgiveness* comes from choosing Thought System #2, the Thought System that leads you to look at the world as a reflection of the ideas in the mind, or *"witness to your state of mind"*, as opposed to something "real" that is taking place outside you.

This makes it a mindset of empowerment instead of a mindset of victimization. You see the world and what takes place in it as *illusory as a dream* – having no substance or power to cause anything. This mindset is the **necessary prerequisite** for practicing *True Forgiveness*.

In the short form of the Introduction of the Text of *A Course In Miracles*, the *Course* uses the analogy of *"a school"* to describe our "presence here". It is a great analogy for understanding the *Course's* perspective of *forgiveness*, so you can then entertain the mindset conducive to *True Forgiveness*.

The following is a practical illustration of the analogy of our life in the world as *"a school"*:

Imagine that the world is a school that you have chosen to attend. So from the moment you wake up in the morning, and even while you sleep at night, you're in school.

Everything that takes place in the world and in your life is part of the curriculum for teaching you what it is you're here to learn.

Everything that comes before you represents different topics, subjects, and classes you have to take.

You will be given assignments, perhaps some lab work, and you might even be asked to work with others in a group setting to complete certain projects.

Neither illness, misfortune, or loss of any kind is unfair or something that "shouldn't" happen or things that happen "to you".

Look at every relationship or situation in which you find yourself as a classroom. Every person, condition or circumstance you encounter is a teaching aid.

Regardless of what seemingly tragic situation takes place in your life, the lives of your loved ones, or those you may not even know in some other part of the world, look at it all as just another opportunity for learning.

What you are learning in every instance is what it is you are accepting to be true for you i.e., which "thought system" you are choosing.

So in any moment or encounter in your life or in the world, when you are not at peace, will be seen as nothing but an opportunity to choose again.

Maintaining the Right Mindset

1. Everything happens in the mind.
2. The way you see and experience anything is not due to the form in which it appears, or the nature of what occurs, but by your state of mind.

These two primary ideas describe the **"Right Mindset"** necessary for the *Consciousness for True Forgiveness*. It's the natural result of looking at your life and the world as "being in school", and seeing every moment as an opportunity for learning.

The *Course's* teaching to *"Beware of the temptation to perceive yourself unfairly treated"* is the guide for recognizing when you're entertaining any of the three major blocks that can thwart your learning:

1. **GUILT**
2. **FEAR**
3. **JUDGMENT**

The moment you experience the slightest form of annoyance, dis-ease, discomfort, or lack of peace, realize it's an indication that you are accepting some thought of *guilt* as real. Remember the acronym stands for the idea that a Godless – Unjust – Insane – Lacking – Tragic thought is real.

Accepting a thought of *guilt* as real is saying that you are accepting the ego's thought system to be true. In doing so you have literally closed off or blocked yourself from recognizing and experiencing the Truth, because you can only experience the nature or content of the thought system you have chosen. *Guilt* leads you to become fearful and feel threatened. False – Evidence – Appearing - Real (FEAR), affirms that the thought of *guilt* is real.

Once you have accepted something to be a real threat, you will naturally engage in some form of *judgment* as to how to protect or defend yourself against that perceived threat.

The following is a series of statements to keep you aware of the Truth or the five metaphysical Facts that are always in operation in every moment, every situation, and every encounter in which you engage. They are to be acknowledged throughout your day, to entertain and maintain the Right Mindset as you go about your activities:

RECOGNIZING THE TRUTH

♦ Let me *be aware* that all that is ever taking place is an out-picturing of the ideas in the mind.

♦ Let me *be aware* that the way I see and experience anything is not because of the form in which it appears, but because of my perception.

♦ Let me *be aware* that every situation or relationship in which I find myself is a *classroom*. Every condition with which I seem to be afflicted is a *teaching aid*; and every person who comes before me is a *forgiveness Partner*.

♦ Let me *be aware* that everything brings me information, inspiration, and instruction, none of which can hurt me and or punish me.

♦ Let me *be aware* that the world is a school and everything that takes place is an opportunity for me to re-learn, recognize, and remember the truth.

Establishing the *Consciousness for True Forgiveness:*

The Following are **SEVEN METAPHYSICAL PREMISES** from *A Course in Miracles* that form the foundation for maintaining the **mindset** for the *Consciousness for True Forgiveness*:

PREMISE #1: "The world is an illusion"

The underlying metaphysical idea is: "Mind is all there is, and the content of the mind is ideas". So all that is ever taking place is your experiencing the ideas in the mind in their truest forms.

Experiencing yourself as a separate individual body living in a world of other separate individual bodies, in different forms is nothing but your experiencing the idea of *"separation"* in its truest form. The world then, is not a geographical place, or a thing. It is the *reflection* of an idea.

PREMISE #2: "Everything is an Idea"

Since mind is all there is, is mind and the content of the mind is ideas, all you are ever dealing with and letting go of is *"an idea or ideas"*. You're never dealing with an event, circumstance, person or condition.

PREMISE #3: "As you think so you experience"

It is your thoughts that determine *"the way or how"* you experience everything that comes into your experience and in your life. The underlying idea: *"Projection makes perception"*. It is your perception, your interpretation, based on your state of mind that determines how you'll "see" and experience anything; not the form, appearance or presence of a person, circumstance or condition.

PREMISE #4: "Feeling unfairly treated in any way means nothing other than you're not identifying with your True Self"

The way you respond in each moment, each encounter with another, or each situation, provides you with information as to what you're accepting to be *"true"* about you.

All feelings of being hurt, offended or victimized in any way are solely because of your belief or identification with your *"body"* as your true identity. *"Bodies"* can be hurt, offended and victimized. But *"you"* are an idea in the mind and ideas can neither hurt nor be hurt.

This is a key premise for forgiving *"yourself"* for the wrong or hurtful things you have accused yourself of *doing*.

PREMISE #5: "To *forgive* is to simply recognize and acknowledge the truth and respond accordingly"

Forgiveness is letting go of the misperception that the *'form'* in which anything appears is real and has power or meaning, or that there is a cause and effect relationship between what you do, have, or experience in the world, and what you feel, who you become, or the quality of your life.

From this perspective: you neither judge nor blame, seek punishment nor restitution, or feel the need for salvation for or from anything or anyone, in any form in the world, and for anything that you feel or experience.

PREMISE #6: "Guilt is nothing other than a false belief you have accepted as "truth"

It's the belief that a godless, unjust, insane, lacking, tragic thought could be "real", and making yourself feel wrong for believing it. For example: In my dream that I shared about earlier, I *believed* what I was dreaming was "real", and what I did in the dream was real, so I woke up feeling *"guilty"* as a natural result of believing what I did (which I really didn't do) was wrong.

PREMISE #7: "In reality, we are only ever doing one of two things: *extending love or calling for love"*

This is the idea that will keep you from feeling personally attacked or taking the words or actions of others *"personally"*, even if there is no doubt that it was directed towards you. This one idea will allow you to realize that the unloving behavior of another is telling you that, in that moment, this person is *"not in their Right Mind"*. In that moment, they are *not aware* of the Truth.

Our true nature is "love" so whenever we're not extending or experiencing love—whether it's because we're feeling unfairly treated or behaving in an unkind or unloving way— we are *"calling for love"*. What this means is that in either case, our only response is *"forgiveness"*, not judgment and punishment. If it is you who are behaving unlovingly, it just means that you, in that moment, are not in your Right Mind and the same response is required—*forgiveness* not *guilt*.

As you can see, *True Forgiveness*—like all everything else the Course teaches—stems from a metaphysical perspective and as a result is supported by metaphysical **"FACTS"**.

The following are the five Key Metaphysical Facts of True Forgiveness:

The 5 METAPHYSICAL FACTS of TRUE FORGIVENESS

FACT #1

Forgiveness is not about absolution or pardon for something done, that is judged to be wrong, but rather about entertaining a perception in which the thought of judgment doesn't come up in the first place.

FACT #2

Forgiveness is not an act or something that takes place between people. It is a "PROCESS" that takes place in the mind that returns the mind to the awareness of the Truth.

FACT #3

In order to practice *forgiveness*, *True Forgiveness*, you must develop the *Consciousness for Forgiveness*. This begins with having the right premise about who you are, where you are, and what is taking place in and as your life and in the world.

FACT #4

All that you are ever letting go of in practicing *True Forgiveness* is a *"mistaken idea"*, never a thing or a condition.

FACT #5

Forgiveness is not a demand made by God or a practice that will make you more "holy" i.e. enlightened or more "spiritual". *Forgiveness* is the means of recognizing and experiencing the Truth, in so doing we experience the Truth in the form of peace and happiness—personally, in our relationships, and in all areas of our lives.

The above **"FACTS"** present a new perspective of *forgiveness* that makes the idea of *forgiveness* appealing, the thought of *forgiving* fearless, and the practice of *forgiveness* simple and pain-free.

These **"FACTS"** establish the Mindset for the consciousness necessary for practicing the **5 STEP TRUE FORGIVENESS PROCESS** that will be taught in the next Chapter.

SECTION III

PRACTISING

TRUE FORGIVENESS

CHAPTER VI

"FROM PAIN TO POWER"

The 5 STEP

TRUE FORGIVENESS PROCESS™

"Certain it is that all distress does not appear to be but unforgiveness.
Yet that's the content underneath the form."
ACIM W-pI.193.4:1

The 5 STEP FORGIVENESS PROCESS I'm about to share, is founded on the following passage from Workbook Lesson 190 in *A Course in Miracles*:

It's your thoughts alone that cause you pain.
Nothing external to your mind can hurt or injure you in
any way.
There is no cause beyond yourself that can reach down
and bring oppression.
No one but yourself affects you.
There is nothing in the world that has the power
to make you ill or sad, weak or frail;
But it is you who have the power to dominate all things
you see,
by merely recognizing what you are.
W-pI.190.5:1-6

I think the word *"pain"* needs to be explained within the context of metaphysics, or from the metaphorical perspective, because taken literally, it can be a little misleading.

Remember the *Course's* central premise that everything happens in the mind, also means that everything is a "thought" or an "idea". *"Pain"* is the reflection or expression of the attempt to accept two opposing thoughts or ideas to be true.

The reason we experience pain in any form is because we are identifying with our bodies, and giving validity and power to all the different forms we see and encounter. We are attempting to make them real or true; and since they are not, we experience the effects of trying to validate two opposing thoughts or ideas.

The Philosophy of True Forgiveness

On page 401 of the Workbook Section of *A Course in Miracles*, in the first paragraph answering the question: *"What Is Forgiveness?"* summarizes the *Course's* entire philosophy of *Forgiveness*. I will give a brief overview of this Passage showing how this philosophy leads to the **5 Step Process of Forgiveness** presented in this Chapter.

The first Paragraph reads:

> *"Forgiveness recognizes that what you thought your brother did to you has not occurred.*
> *It does not pardon sins and make them real.*
> *It sees there was no sin.*
> *And in that view, are all your sins forgiven.*
> *What is sin, except a false idea about God's Son?*
> *Forgiveness merely sees its falsity, and therefore lets it go.*
> *What then is free to take its place is now the Will of God."*
> **(W-pII.1.1:1-7)**

The first two lines: *"Forgiveness recognizes that what you thought your brother did to you has not occurred."* **(W-pII.1.1:1)**

This reflects the *Course's* perspective that nothing ever happens *"to"* you. This does not mean that someone may not have said, or done something un-loving that was directed towards you; or on which you were on the receiving end. However, those un-loving words or actions were **not** the cause of any lack of peace, or pain you may be feeling.

Forgiveness then is recognizing that there is no *"cause-and-effect"* relationship between what you experience and what you feel.

These next three lines: ***"It does not pardon sins and make them real. It sees there was no sin. And in that view are all your sins forgiven."***
(W-pII.1.1:2-4)

These lines directly reflect the *Consciousness for True Forgiveness* because from that consciousness, nothing is judged as being a "sin". A "sin" is something that can affect "Reality" i.e. affect the Truth of the way things are in some way. Since the world and its effects are as illusory as a dream, nothing that takes place here is real or has any effect. From this perspective then – no sin was committed so there's no sin to be pardoned.

Within the *Consciousness for True Forgiveness* nothing really happens so harm is never done. Just like *"dreaming of stealing the cash I had found"*, did not make me guilty of theft when I awoke, because it was *"just a dream"*. There was no need for me to feel guilty, because I had not committed a crime.

The last three lines: *"What is sin except a false idea about God's Son? Forgiveness merely sees its falsity, and therefore lets it go. What then is free to take its place is now the Will of God."* (W-pII.1.1:5-7)

These last lines can be seen as reflecting the *Course's* perspective of why we experience the myriad pain and problems we have in the world; and why or how *True Forgiveness* is the means to healing, and the solution to all our problems.

The first of these three lines: *"What is sin, except a false idea about God's Son?"* refers to the Course's following perspective of problems: *All problems are problems of perception, or rather misperception, stemming from misunderstanding or lack of awareness of the truth.*

All the pain and problems we experience in the world begin with our misunderstanding or lack of awareness of the Truth of who we are and what is taking place.

The second line: *"Forgiveness merely sees its falsity and therefore lets it go."* refers to what happens when you develop the *Consciousness for True Forgiveness.*

In so doing you will automatically experience the last line: *"What then is left to take its place is now the Will of God."* The *"Will of God."* is a metaphor for: the truth, reality, peace, oneness, all that is opposite to pain, problems, conflict, separation, or that does not reflect the underlying unchangeable metaphysical Truth.

This paragraph suggests that *True Forgiveness* is really a process of recognizing, realizing and accepting the truth. In so doing, we correct our perception and transform a painful experience.

The 5 STEP FORGIVENESS PROCESS

Workbook Lesson 134 in *A Course In Miracles* titled, *"Let me perceive forgiveness as it is"*, the *Course* offers a step-by-step guide of sorts, for understanding *True Forgiveness* and how to practice. It implies that in its most basic form, the inner process that results in the experience of *forgiveness* can be likened to engaging in an inner conversation.

The content of the inner conversation that leads to the experience of *forgiveness* is like a line of reasoning, recognizing and acknowledging thoughts or ideas of truth, and dismissing thoughts of fear, guilt, and judgment.

Keep in mind that it is the content of your inner conversation that is then experienced in different forms. Just to illustrate, take look at the different content of the inner conversations reflected in the following Acronyms: "P-A-I-N" - "P-E-A-C-E" and "P-O-W-E-R"

P ~ A ~ I ~ N

P
You take whatever is said, done or takes place PERSONALLY i.e. as a personal attack or something that has or is being done "to you" and as a result believe it will affect you in some way.

A
You ATTRIBUTE everything you feel and the way you experience anything to what happened – the specific form, along with your happiness, peace of mind, and the quality of your life to what you do, have and experience in your life, and in the world.

I
You IDENTIFY yourself by and with your body, personality, and your experiences, accomplishments, abilities, etc., and you believe that they are what defines you.

N
NOT BEING open or WILLING to consider there might be another way or approach to looking at or responding to the form or appearance of what takes place in your life and in the world. You judge according to appearances.

P ~ E ~ A ~ C ~ E

P
You're willing to PRACTICE FORGIVING in response to every situation and as a way of life.

E
You EXTEND and EXPRESS only love regardless of circumstance.

A
You ACKNOWLEDGE and accept only thoughts of truth to guide you.

C
You CHOOSE to address the true cause of your feelings in any situation rather than blaming something or someone outside you.

E
You ENTERTAIN the perspective that nothing comes to hurt you rather, everything is a learning opportunity.

P ~ O~ W ~ E ~ R

P
You are aware that all that is taking place in and as your life and in myriad forms in the world is nothing other than your experiencing the idea of separation through the PRINCIPLE of PROJECTION.

O
Look at every moment, situation, or condition in which you are not at peace as an OPPORTUNITY to remember the truth and, in so doing, see it from the perspective of love instead of fear.

W
Remember that what you are feeling in any given moment or towards another is the result of WHAT YOU ARE TELLING YOURSELF to be true, and never caused by the person, situation, or anything that's occurring in that moment.

E
Choose to EXPERIENCE ONLY PEACE as the outcome in every situation, circumstance or condition.

R
RECOGNIZE that what you feel will always depend on what you are making REAL in your mind. RECOGNIZE that you always and only experience the effects of your thoughts. RECOGNIZE that there is nothing, other than you, that has any power over you.

The 5 STEP PROCESS is as follows:

STEP 1: Recognize and identify with your True Self.

STEP 2: Be aware of the truth of what is taking place every moment and in every situation.

STEP 3: Realize and acknowledge that it's not what happens but the way you look at it that determines the way you experience *anything*.

STEP 4: Make the choice or decision for peace in every instance, situation or circumstance.

STEP 5: Recognize that the only solution to pain or problems is *forgiveness*.

These 5 STEPS depend on an inner conversation that consists of:

- AWARENESS
- NON-JUDGMENT
- TRUE PERCEPTION
- THE DESIRE FOR PEACE
- ACCEPTANCE

PRACTICING THE 5 STEP PROCESS

This PROCESS consists of TWO PARTS:

PART I: Recognizing you are entertaining a Misperception
PART II: Being willing to correct that perception

STEP 1: Recognize and identify with your True Self

Recognize any moment or situation in which you're not at peace. Feeling unfairly treated or victimized in any way is because you are perceiving yourself falsely.

STEP #1 is vitally important because:
1) It is the one lesson we're here to learn.
2) Identifying with our *True Self* is what will allow us to remain empowered and at peace when faced with circumstances or conditions that appear threatening.

If you were to take a look at what you're telling yourself in any moment or situation in which you feel victimized in any way, you will always find that you're telling yourself a story about how what is being said or done is taking you off your peace, or negatively affecting you in some way.

Recognize and acknowledge the following idea:

"I am not the victim of the world I see."
ACIM W-pI.31

The opening line of this workbook lesson says it all: *"Today's idea is the introduction to your declaration of release"*. This idea brings release, the moment you accept the idea that you can never be victimized by anything or anyone.

Allen Watson is a highly regarded and reputable teacher and practitioner of the teachings of A Course in Miracles, now retired from *Circle of Atonement Teaching and Healing Center*. *Allen Watson*, also a prolific writer once wrote an article titled: *"A New Way of Looking at Yourself"*.

In this article he describes an image of our *"True Self"* based on the perspective of A Course in Miracles – the perspective of Truth. As *Allen Watson* says by way of introduction to the article: *"As you read these words imagine "God" is speaking these words to you, about you, i.e. telling, describing, **His** vision of you".*

With permission from *The Circle of Atonement* to use this article, I am using it, almost in its entirety as the **Process** for practicing this very important **STEP**. I have made only a few minor word changes, just to keep it consistent with the terminology used in this book.

GUIDED PROCESS FOR RECOGNIZING YOUR TRUE SELF

A New Way of Looking at Yourself

There is nothing wrong with you. There is nothing bad about you, nothing twisted or spoiled. You really are the innocent child of God.

You have looked at what you are, at thoughts you have had, at certain ways you have felt, and you have said, "You are a bad person!"

You have thought what you saw in yourself was ugly and black, or pitiful and weak, or—worst of all—hopeless. You have judged yourself horribly and unmercifully.
I have good news for you. You were wrong!

It is so very, very hard to admit you were wrong, even about something as awful as this. Feeling this way about yourself is the only thing you know, the only way of 'being' that you know.

You identify with it. It is comfortable, somehow - even in its perverted sickness. Somehow you feel, "This is me. I'm at home with this. I'm afraid to even think I am anything else, anything better, because I would feel terribly, profoundly disappointed if I dared to hope, and then found out I'd been right in the first place.

Better not to hope. Better not to dream that maybe, somehow, in some magical way, I might be innocent instead of guilty."

And yet you are wrong. The guilt you feel is without cause; nothing happened. You didn't sin. Not ever!

Oh, you did those things you remember. You said those awful words. The person you loved does indeed feel hurt, and hurt by you. We can't deny that.

What we can deny, though—what I and the Holy Spirit and God the Father deny—is that those things you feel so guilty about mean what you think they mean.

They do not mean you are evil.
They do not mean that you have "sinned."
They do not mean that you are cut off from God forever, or even for the tiniest tick of time.
They do not mean that you have somehow lost your innocence, which was given you as a gift of God in creation.
They do not mean that you are no longer a loving being.
They do not mean you are unworthy of love, unworthy of grace, unworthy of God's gifts, unworthy of health or life or abundance.
They do not mean you are no longer entitled to joy.
They do not mean you are damned.
They do not mean that anything of value has been lost or hurt or damaged.

You have been seeing your own thoughts, words and actions and deeming them to be sin, to be proof that you are no longer a child of God. And you have been wrong. I rejoice to tell you, you have been wrong! What God created holy cannot be corrupted.

It's all a matter of interpretation, you see.

These things that shame you that make you feel so small, these dark secrets that you have never shared with another soul, or often wish you had never shared—you have looked at these things and judged them as "sin." What a silly idea! They are not "sins" at all. That's just a foolish notion you have had; a foolish notion that has played havoc with the world as you see it.

Because so much of what you have judged as dark and evil in yourself is unbearable— and there is so very, very much that you have judged in yourself—you have striven to project it outside yourself. You react violently when you think you see these things in other people because you are so very, very afraid to admit that those same dark thoughts exist in yourself.

What you do not like in another is what you are afraid to see in yourself.
But you are afraid for no reason. These things in you are not "sin." That is only an interpretation that you have made, and it is an interpretation that is wholly unfounded. You have grossly undervalued yourself. You have misjudged yourself.

You attacked your brothers only because you believed you were deprived by them of something you needed.
In reality you were never deprived at all; your attack came from ignorance. It was a mistake, not a sin. You can learn this about yourself by learning it about your brothers. When they appear to attack you, they are offering you a chance to bless yourself by blessing them—by seeing past the appearance of their ego to the reality of who they truly are.

You feel lack in yourself because you insist on seeing lack in your brothers, and what you deny to them you deny to yourself. You can't love yourself as your ego sees you, but you can realize that the ego, and the ego's picture of you, is not you at all. All you need to do is to deny the reality of this false, unloving self in your brothers.

I have said, "Teach no one that he is what you would not want to be". (T-7.VII.3:8). As long as you continue to see evil in them, you will see it in yourself. Teach them, instead, of their True Self as God's Sons, and you will remember your own True Self.

You have been caught up in an insane whirlwind of self-judgment and self-loathing. How very wrong you have been! You are the innocent and beloved child of God.

You are an extension and expression of God, which is love.
Love is all there is.
*Love is what you **know** to be right, what you **know** to be true, what you know to be good and holy and pure.*
*And you know that because **that is what you are**.*

*How awfully, terribly frustrating it has been all your life, to **know** what you **ought** to be, and to feel you never could **be** that! How sad, how tragic your life has felt!*

Dear brother! Dear sister! Rejoice! For you have made no more than a foolish mistake! You are not the pitiful being you thought you were.

Your dark secrets are not sins. They are not weaknesses. They are not failures.

What you thought of as "sins" are nothing but your misperceptions and they are not your damnation; they are your salvation.

You are still an idea in the Mind of God. You have never separated from God, and you are still just as you were created to be. Nothing has changed. You can be what you always knew you should be! You already are. You have never ceased being exactly that!

*There are only two emotions, love and fear, and fear is nothing but a call for love. Abandon your self-judgment. Let go of that self-doubt. Remove the crown of thorns and stop hammering in the nails; you are not guilty! You **are not guilty!** You do not deserve this crucifixion! God did not will this for you! You have chosen it for yourself. And it need not be!*

*When you are able to look at every awful thing you have judged in yourself and see the truth about it - that it is nothing but your confused mind calling for love – because it has mistakenly believed there could be something "other" than love - you will **recognize** your True Self.*

STEP 2: Be aware of the truth of what is taking place every moment and in every situation.

Recognize that all things are neutral. Seeing anything in and of itself as bad, wrong, sinful or as the cause of pain or distress is the result of your own judgment.

Be mindful of the fact that the way you see and experience anything is based solely on your perception – the way you look at something and the interpretation you make about it. There is no inherent meaning or power in the "form" in which anything appears.

Recognize this fact and acknowledge the following idea:

"I am never upset for the reason I think."
ACIM W-pI.5

What this means, is that a person may very well be behaving in an un-kind, un-loving, or even disparaging manner; and a situation or condition might be uncomfortable or even life threatening, but neither the occurrence nor presence of either of those is the cause of your feelings of hurt, worry or fear.

What you are seeing and experiencing is the result of your state of mind—the Thought System you're accepting as the Truth.

Entertain the following Ideas daily to remind you and maintain your awareness of the Truth of what is taking place in every moment and every situation:

RECOGNIZING THE TRUTH

Let me *be aware* that all that is ever taking place is an out-picturing of the ideas in the mind.

Let me *be aware* that the way I see and experience anything is not because of the form in which it appears, but because of my perception.

Let me *be aware* that every situation or relationship in which I find myself is a *classroom*. Every condition with which I seem to be afflicted is a *teaching aid*; and every person who comes before me is a *Forgiveness Partner*.

Let me *be aware* that everything brings me information, inspiration, and instruction none of which can hurt me and or punish me.

Let me *be aware* that the world is a school and everything that takes place is an opportunity for me to re-learn, recognize, and remember the truth.

STEP 3: Realize and acknowledge that's it's not what happens but what you're telling yourself about it that determines the way you experience *anything*.

Recognize that you will always and only experience the contents of your thoughts in some form.

This means that, it is as you think, so you experience. The pain you're experiencing— whether it is in the form of worry, guilt, fear, and being unfairly treated—is the *expression in form* of the thoughts of judgment, against that (other) person or thing to which you are pointing an accusing finger i.e. judging.

You are experiencing the exact nature of the story you're telling yourself about how the actions, behavior, situation, and presence of a condition, have affected you, or is affecting you in a painful way.

Recognize and acknowledge the following idea:

"It's your thoughts alone that cause you pain."
ACIM W-pI.190.5:1

This idea is pivotal and the key to letting go of your pain. It helps you to realize that when you judge and condemn another, you are also judging and condemning yourself. This keeps you holding on to the very pain you want to release. Realizing that it is the thoughts of judgment you're holding that is the sole cause of your pain, you also realize that by simply releasing those thoughts, you release the pain you're feeling.

Practicing this STEP requires the willingness to recognize you're telling yourself a *Story of pain*; recognize it's the content of your *Story* that you're experiencing in the form of pain; and be willing to release it and become open to a new perspective – a perspective of Truth.

Telling Your Story

You can guide yourself through this process or you can have an Accessing Inner Wisdom Counselor or Inner Guidance Counselor guide you into a completely relaxed state, so you can connect with your own Inner Wisdom, (See http://www.pathwaysoflight.org for a listing of *Accessing Inner Wisdom Counselors*)

To guide yourself through this Process: Find a quiet comfortable place where you won't be disturbed. Allow yourself about 30 – 45 minutes just so you don't feel rushed, but take whatever time you need until you feel complete.

Get into a completely relaxed state. You can use a Guided Audio; guide yourself mentally; or do a total Body Relaxation routine.

When you feel completely relaxed turn your attention towards the pain you're feeling:

1. Without justification or explanation, examine and tell your story truthfully: Look at the meaning you're giving to the situation; interpretations and assumptions you're making; what you are afraid or worried about; what judgments you've made...
2. Acknowledge what you are feeling and experiencing without guilt or judgment...
3. Realize that what you are feeling and experiencing in the form of pain is simply the content of those thoughts, and since they are only thoughts, you can change or release them...
4. You can then envision yourself releasing those thoughts in some way: perhaps seeing them as a thought bubble that you burst or blow away, or that simply dissolves; or mentally acknowledging those thoughts to be untrue; or some other way that works for you...
5. Then ask for *Inner Guidance* in looking at, and entertaining thoughts about your *Story of Pain*. This process will allow you to re-tell your

Story from a perspective of peace instead of pain...

STEP 4: Make the choice or decision for peace in every instance, situation or circumstance.

Recognize that letting go of your thoughts of judgment, is simply being willing to consider another way of looking at the person or thing you have been judging.

This reinforces the idea that it is not what happens but the way you look at it that determines the way you experience anything.

This is where your power lies. Power is not something you have or don't have, or something that can be taken away from you. Power is what you experience when you make the choice for peace in any moment or situation.

Recognize this truth and acknowledge the following idea:

"I could see peace instead of this."
ACIM W-pI.34

Be aware that peace, or experiencing peace is not the result of being in a peaceful place or engaging in some form of activity to bring you peace. In truth, peace is the result of *choosing a peaceful outcome*, or wanting the experience of peace to be your only choice in any given situation. The Course teaches: *"Every choice is a choice for peace, or nothing"*.

The following is a brief guided process for choosing peace. It's a process that can return you to a state of peace almost the instant you recognize you're not at peace. It's aptly titled:

I WANT TO EXPERIENCE PEACE

I want to see this differently.
(Whatever the "THIS" is)
I want to see this as it really is.
I am open to a new perspective—a perspective that
brings me peace.
I want to be at peace. I want to see peace
instead of what I now see.
So I remind myself that peace is a choice that I must make,
if I want to see this differently; and that peace is a choice
I can make.
So in this moment, I willingly make that choice because I
want to
see peace instead of this.

STEP 5: Recognize that the only solution to pain or problems is forgiveness.

Recognize *forgiveness* as your function.

Remember that *forgiving*, from the perspective of truth, means to look past and dismiss the illusory forms of everything you see and experience in the world.

As your "function" then, *forgiveness* is the way you are to respond to every perception of threat or victimization to remind you of the Truth that none of it is real.

The idea to recognize and acknowledge is the following central course idea:

"Seek not to change the world, but choose to change your mind
about the world."
ACIM T-21.in.1:7

This is what you are doing when you are *forgiving*. You are choosing to change your mind about the reality of the world. You're recognizing and acknowledging the truth.

This is the one lesson the *Course* intends to teach, and the one lesson we're here to learn. The short form of the Introduction to the Text of *A Course in Miracles* that opens with the statement: *"This is a course in miracles."* The following lines in its closing paragraph supports this intention in saying this:

"The course does not aim at teaching the meaning of love,
for that is beyond what can be taught. It does aim,
however, at removing the blocks to the awareness of love's
presence, which is your natural inheritance." (T-in.1:6-7)

Course Base Forgiveness — *True Forgiveness* — is the means by which you remove "the blocks to the awareness of love's presence". Those "blocks" are the misperceptions that something other than love exists; i.e. that there is something that could block or prevent you experiencing love.

What will allow you to practice this STEP, i.e. recognize *forgiveness* as the answer to pain and problems and as your "function", is changing your mind about the world as a place you come into and, in which things happen *"to you"*.

Accept and entertain the analogy of the world as a school; your presence "here" is a required course and everything you experience is necessary to help you learn, what it is you're "here" to learn. *Forgiveness* then will simply become your natural response to everyone and in every situation.

In the next chapter, I will share a **BLUEPRINT FOR HAPPINESS** based on the Course's central teachings and ideas for practicing True *Forgiveness.*

CHAPTER VII

THE

"BLUEPRINT FOR HAPPINESS"

"Forgiveness is the key to happiness."
ACIM W-pI.121

During the early 90's, before I heard of *A Course in Miracles*, I was very involved in self-help and personal development. Like many others, I too thought that by working on myself, my relationships, and changing the circumstances in my life, I would feel happy and fulfilled.

I had a friend at the time who also shared the same perspective and we would talk about this frequently over the phone, and during our lunches and dinners. We would discuss the latest self-help book we'd been reading, share helpful tips and insights we learned with each other, talk about where we were on our path that day, and what our last derailment was.

A frequent topic of conversation was the fact that no matter how much we seemed to be working on ourselves, our relationships and our lives, we couldn't seem to get to that happy and fulfilled place for any extended period of time.

Oh we had our moments. As a matter of fact we had so many moments, "emotional rollercoaster" was the term that at the time seemed to define both our lives.

During one of our conversations my friend said: *"You know, there are all kinds of 12 Step programs for people with addictions, disorders, and what is considered to be some type of dysfunction; but there isn't anything like that for people like us who, by all appearances are 'normal', but nevertheless feel very dysfunctional. Wouldn't it be nice if there was a 12 Step program for people like us? We may not have what is considered a socially unaccepted addiction, an obvious disorder or a diagnosed dysfunction but we suffer from the same lack of fulfillment, unhappiness and inner turmoil that the people with those conditions do; and that the 12 Step programs are designed to heal."*

I remember thinking at the time that it was a most *"brilliant idea"* and that *"brilliant idea"*, never left my mind. Years later when I became professionally involved in personal development, I know somewhere in the back of my mind there was this "unspoken intention" to discover, create or develop a sort of *"12 Step program"* for people like my friend and me, who seemed to be suffering with what I have termed *a "Socially Accepted Dysfunctional Disorder"*. It even carries the most appropriate acronym: *"SADD"*.

Well all these years later I have finally found it in the teaching of *A Course in Miracles* that says: *"Forgiveness is the key to happiness."* Remember, from the perspective of the *Course*, all our problems and unhappiness stem from misperceptions. The *Course* therefore presents *True Forgiveness* as the solution, correcting our misperceptions.

Using the Acronym: **"T(rue)-F-O-R-G-I-V-E-N-E-S-S"** I have created a **"BLUEPRINT FOR HAPPINESS"**. It shows you how to practice the 12 Central Lessons, honoring the underlying metaphysical Truths and correcting your perception.

This **BLUEPRINT** provides you with the metaphorical *"key to happiness"*.

THE BLUEPRINT FOR HAPPINESS

"T"
TAKE RESPONSIBILITY for the choices you make and the quality of life you experience.

Henry David Thoreau said: *"When you advance confidently in the direction of your dreams, and endeavor to live the life you imagined you will meet with success unexpected in common hours."*

A problem for many people is that of feeling unfulfilled and unsuccessful, because they do not advance confidently in the direction of their dreams, and don't even think they *"could"* live the life, they have imagined.

This is because they see themselves as products of their environment, seeing their upbringing, circumstances and conditions, as the determiner of what they are capable of or what they deserve to experience.

Holding this misperception will lead to being unhappy and unfulfilled in two ways:

1) If you did not have an "ideal" childhood or family life— felt you weren't exposed to the right opportunities or disadvantaged in some way—you will hold yourself back from doing what you feel *"called"* to do because you doubt your abilities. You will not as Thoreau said, *"...advance confidently in the direction of your dreams..."*

2) On the other hand if you feel disadvantaged or not "up to par", you will make life, and relationship choices, that you believe will give you the credibility, validity or the worthiness you think you lack. These choices

however may not at all in alignment with what you feel *"called"* to do, and you will end up feeling empty and unfulfilled regardless of what, or how much you achieve or accomplish.

ACIM LESSON: "There's another way of looking at the world."
(W-pI.33)

The above *Course* lesson is teaching the underlying Truth that it's not what happens, but the way you look at it that determines the way you experience anything.

Be aware that metaphorically *"the world"* refers to whatever it is you have "set apart" in your mind and are giving attention to in any given moment or situation. So it's not the specifics of your childhood, circumstances or conditions that determine what you deserve or are capable of, but your looking at it as if it was.

The truth is you are *not* the product of your environment. Nothing or no one is the determiner of who you become, what you're capable of, or what you deserve. Regardless of your past or present circumstances you are free to choose the way you experience it, simply by changing the way you look at it.

"F"
Focus on the FACTS of what is taking place, not your feelings.

The misperception here is similar to the one above but this one goes a step further. It suggests that it *"is"* what happens that determines the way you experience it, because events circumstances and people *"are"* the cause of your feelings.

If you've ever felt your day, a moment, or the way you were experiencing something changed because of something someone said or did, or by "what happened" you're holding this misperception.

This is the misperception that will make you feel like people are always "pushing your buttons", and your happiness and peace of mind will be dependent on circumstances, events and the way you're treated by others.

ACIM LESSON: "I am never upset for the reason I think." (W-pI.5)

Remember, it's not what happens but how you look at it that determines the way you experience it. What you feel in any situation is based on your perception, and perception is interpretation, not "FACT".

The fact that something has occurred does not mean it will affect you in any specific way. Whenever you feel upset, angry or hurt by anything that has occurred, it is only because you're telling yourself that what has occurred is the cause of your feelings.

This Course Lesson is reminding you that you're never upset, hurt or angry by what happens outside you, but only because of the way you are *"looking"* at what is outside you.

Be aware that the only determiner of the way you feel is *"you"* because it is your perception that leads to what you experience.

"O"
Look at any seemingly painful experience, situation or encounter as a learning OPPORTUNITY.

Another commonly held misperception is that life is unfair and illness, misfortune or any form of painful experience, are some form of punishment coming from God or the universe.

But the *Course's* analogy is: *The world is a school and everything that comes before you is part of the curriculum.* So the Truth is, regardless of the situation in which you find yourself or what you may encounter, you're in school. You may not recognize the lesson or you may find it difficult or confusing, but see nothing that comes into your experience as coming to hurt you.

ACIM LESSON: "All things are lessons God would have me learn."
(W-pI.193)

This lesson is teaching you to look at everything as bringing you information, inspiration, and instruction so that you feel neither persecuted, nor punished by anything that takes place.

This will help you realize that nothing comes to hurt you; rather everything serves the purpose of teaching you which thought system you're accepting as true. It will make you aware that everything happens in the mind; so you can change any experience of being unfairly treated simply by changing your mind, by changing the thought system you are accepting as true.

"R"
REMIND yourself that the world, everything that takes place in the world, and everything that takes place in your life, is nothing but the reflection or projection, of an idea in the mind.

The unquestionable, collective misperception we all hold, is that the world is a place in which we are born into—in which we live—and what we do, have, and experience in the world can make or break us. We see our lives as a constant struggle of "us against the world".

This misperception if not corrected is what will lead you to feel unfairly treated, or persecuted whenever you experience any form of illness, misfortune or loss.

Remember the world is really nothing but an *"idea"*. It is the idea of separation that is being experienced in its truest form, and ideas cannot hurt, attack, nor *cause* any effect.

ACIM LESSON: "I am not the victim of the world I see." (W-pI.31)

This is one of the most liberating *Course* lessons because as the title suggests, you are never at the mercy of, nor affected in any real way, by anything that you see or experience in the world.

This one awareness can radically transform the quality of your experience in all areas of your life. Imagine entering relationships, and pursuing your dreams and all endeavors, without fear. Imagine nothing that you encounter or experience, can cause you hurt, harm or loss; or leave you *"scarred for life"* in some way.

Remind yourself that you can never be victimized by anything you do, have, or experience in the world, because the *"world"* is literally nothing but an idea in your mind.

"G"
GIVE UP the misperception that anything happens "to" you.

When you accept the ego's thought system that says the world is real, you will see everything that takes place your life as happening *"to"* you.

This is the misperception that leads you to worry about all the possible 'bad' things that can happen *"to"* you. This is also what causes you to take things "personally", finding yourself frequently and/or easily offended. This will always have you feeling fearful, and disrupt your peace of mind.

ACIM LESSON: "Fear is not justified in any form." (W-pII.240)

This lesson teaches that there is nothing to fear, subtly reminding you that the world is *"the witness to your state of mind"*, i.e. like a mirror image reflecting the contents of your mind. A mirror image has neither power nor substance regardless of the *form* in which it appears, so it can do nothing to anything or anyone.

As a reflection or mirror image of your state of mind, nothing you experience *"here"* happens *"to"* you, but *"through"* you— through the perceptions you hold and interpretations you make about the world.

"I"
Always and only IDENTIFY with your true Self.

We generally identify with our body, gender, nationality, etc., and we are encouraged to define ourselves by our accomplishments and what we see as special gifts, talents, or abilities.

This misperception is the cause of all feelings of insecurity, unworthiness, low self-esteem, lack of confidence, fear of success and fear of failure, as well as difficulty building and sustaining relationships.

When you identify yourself as your *"body"* or by any attributes or characteristics, you will always see yourself as vulnerable and lacking in some way. You will then look for ways to feel safe or more worthy, and to compensate for your perceived lack.

This can lead to engaging in unhealthy behaviors and relationships such as addictions and other abusive situations, worsening your self-image and increasing your feelings of unworthiness.

ACIM LESSON: "I am not a body. I am free." (W-pI.199)

This lesson is teaching us how to perceive ourselves correctly so we can identify with our *"True Self"* which is complete, worthy, capable; and can never be changed, affected or defiled by any experience.

Identifying with your *True Self* will allow you to let go of those fears that keep you from acting on the desires of your heart or sabotaging your progress so you can't seem to follow through with your goals and dreams, to completion.

"V"
Accept a new VISION of happiness as changing your perception instead of changing circumstances or conditions

A primary source of unhappiness is the belief that happiness comes from having the right relationship, career, lifestyle, money, good health etc., in other words, happiness is seen as dependent on circumstance.

This is another misperception, that by its very nature will keep us unhappy and in pain, because it reinforces the belief that the world is "real" and we are "victims" of it. We firmly believe that we must have certain things, or things must be a certain way in order for us to be happy.

ACIM LESSON: "Forgiveness ends the dream of suffering here."
(W-pII.333)

This lesson teaches why *"Forgiveness is the key to happiness."* The *Course* describes our experience here as *"dreaming a dream"*. This means that everything here is *"illusory"*. *"Forgiveness"* is defined as seeing past the illusory forms and recognizing the truth that lies behind, in other words, recognizing it's all a dream.

By practicing *True Forgiveness* you wake up from the dream, realizing that your happiness is neither affected nor determined by anything you do, have or experience in the dream.

"E"
Choose always to EXPERIENCE only peace as your desired outcome in every situation.

Most of us agonize when it comes to making choices and decisions. We know we have made the right choice or decision when we feel peaceful as a result. We agonize and find decision-making difficult because we think that it is "what" we choose that will determine whether it's the right choice, or what will make us feel peaceful.

ACIM LESSON: "I could see peace instead of this." (W-pI.34)

This lesson teaches that "peace" must be *what* you choose as our desired outcome or experience, in order to experience peace. It is not a specific form or set of circumstances that will bring you peace.

I came to understand this personally when I made a decision a few years ago that was logically sound, practical, benefited everyone involved, and was the most loving choice at the time. By all appearances, it was perfect. Shortly after however, I found I was having these underlying feelings of guilt, that I just couldn't understand because, given the circumstances, I should have experienced nothing but peace.

Upon examination, I realized that even though I would make the same choice or decision all over again, my underlying motivation was *"defense"*.

Examine your underling motives in every decision you make. Remember you will always and only experience the contents of your thoughts. When your choice is to experience peace, without conditions or an agenda, whatever decision you make will feel peaceful because "peace" will be the content of your thoughts.

"N"
NOTICE that any moment or situation in which you are in pain or not at peace is because you're trying to make something "real" that isn't.

We're always engaged in an inner conversation that is based on one of the two thought systems. Any situation or encounter with which you're not at peace is solely because you're engaged in an inner conversation that is affirming the ego's thought system that says the world is "real".

This will always make you fearful because if the world is real, you are a victim. The content of your inner conversation will consist of ways to protect or defend yourself against the perceived world of attack and you will experience it in some form of fear.

ACIM LESSON: "Truth will correct all the errors in my mind." (W-pI.107)

This lesson reminds you that there's another thought system, redirecting your mind to the truth. By noticing the true cause of your pain or lack of peace in any moment, situation or encounter, you automatically become aware of the truth. Acknowledging and accepting the truth is recognizing and accepting only what is real.

"E"
Choose to EXTEND and EXPRESS ONLY LOVE in every moment, situation, or encounter.

"Judgment" is declaring something to be separate or different based on its form, appearance or behavior. It stems from the misperception that we are always *threatened* by what goes on in the world, and "judgment" is a way to defend and protect ourselves.

Because the world is the reflection of the idea of separation, "judgment", is really just another form in which this idea is being expressed and experienced.

ACIM LESSON: "Judgment and love are opposites." (W-pII.352)

This lesson makes it quite clear: if you're not extending or expressing love, you're engaging in judgment.

Extending and Expressing love is about allowing, accepting and letting all things be *without* judgment or conditions. It is the awareness and understanding that you cannot be threatened by anything or anyone, and it will always be experienced in a feeling of peace, safety and freedom.

"S"
Realize that the pain and problems you experience is all just your STORY.

The *Course* describes the world as, *"...the witness to your state of mind, the outside picture of an inward condition."* (T-21.in:I.5)
The pain and problems we experience in the world is the reflection of a *"story"* based on the made up belief that we are a "body", living in a world consisting of other bodies, that can hurt, affect and have power over us, "our body", in various ways.

What this means is that all illness, disappointment, seeming setbacks, loss and even death are nothing but the playing out of the script of a *"story of victimization"*, that we are telling ourselves in our mind—the witness to our state of mind.

ACIM LESSON: "I loose the world from all I thought it was".
(W-pI.132)

This lesson presents another extremely liberating and empowering perspective. Resting on the awareness that the world I experience is the result of the way I think about it in my mind, it suggests that I can simply *"loose"* —let go of— those thoughts and I will be fine.

In its simplest form, this is what *A Course in Miracles* wants us to learn and it is summed up clearly and succinctly in one of the *Course's* most central teachings:

> *"Seek not to change the world, but choose*
> *to change our minds about the world."*

Whatever I experience, it's just *"my story"* and I am free to tell it differently.

"S"
Let go of the misperception that anything *"SHOULDN'T BE"*.

We firmly believe that we are entitled to a perfect pain-free life. The moment something seems even slightly painful we find it's unfair, and we think it shouldn't be. This is because from our perspective everything *"does not"* happen in the mind. We believe that what we experience is what is done *"to"* us, by sources other than us.

As a result of that same misperception we believe that a *"miracle"*, is an extraordinary occurrence also coming from a source other than us, that would save us from those undeserving things that *"happen to us"*.

ACIM IDEA: "I am entitled to miracles." (W-pI.77)

This lesson clears up the two major misperceptions that are in operation here:

First, the *Course* re-defines the miracle as a *"change in perception"* rather than a change in conditions.

Second, it reminds you that it's not what happens, but the way you look at it that determines the way you experience anything. This is the thought of truth that will correct the misperception that you can *ever* be unfairly treated, or that you are entitled to a perfect pain-free life.

The awareness that you are entitled to miracles allows you to let go of the misperception that anything *"SHOULDN'T BE"*, because you realize that regardless of what seems to come into your life, how it affects you rests solely on the way you choose to look at it.

As you will note, the lessons creating this **BLUEPRINT** *(the same lessons that form the framework for True Forgiveness)* are very similar in content and reflect the same idea: ***"You are not the victim of the world you see."***

Entertaining this idea *is* the key to happiness because it will change your perception, helping you realize that you're dreaming a dream, and the dream that you're dreaming is false.

In the following closing section, I leave you with a **Practice** for making *True Forgiveness* a part of your daily life.

CONCLUSION

Beyond the Words to the Meaning

"But the only meaningful prayer is for forgiveness, because those who have been forgiven have everything."
ACIM T-3.V.6:3

In Chapter 16 in *A Course in Miracles*, the last paragraph of Section VII aptly entitled, **"The End of Illusions"**, closes with the following words written in the form of a prayer.

Metaphorically, to *"pray"* is to join your mind with God's. To join your mind with God's simply means to recognize and acknowledge this truth:

- Love and God, are one
- Love/God is all there is; you are one with love/God
- Only love/God is real

True Forgiveness—recognizing and acknowledging the Truth—is the ultimate "form" of joining your mind with God's. It gives rise to a *Consciousness for True Forgiveness*. Entertaining this type of consciousness will allow you to feel complete, whole, unthreatened and unaffected regardless of circumstances, conditions or appearances.

This is the meaning of the words in the above quote and why it says: *"...those who have been forgiven have everything."*
The closing line of the paragraph that precedes the passage that is called the *"Forgiveness Prayer"* says that in every moment or situation, *"you choose this or nothing."*
The, this, to which it's referring to, is the choice for *True Forgiveness*.

I will close with this "Prayer" and share with you a **"Guided Meditative Process"**, derived from this "Prayer". This guided process will help you make the choice for *"everything instead of nothing"*, by preparing you to respond with *forgiveness* instead of *judgment* throughout your day.

First I'd like to share with you a few helpful tips for using the "Prayer" and the guided process most effectively. Then I will share the "Prayer" followed by the guided process.

WHEN TO USE THE PRAYER AND/OR THE PROCESS

1) At the beginning and end of each day
2) Whenever you're feeling victimized or unfairly treated in any way
3) When you don't know how to respond to a situation you find troubling
4) If you're having difficulty letting go of any/or all of the following:
   - anger
   - bitterness
   - judgment
   - any form of Fear
   - being betrayed
   - being abused in any way
   - being dismissed, disrespected, ignored: like you don't matter
   - guilt
   - feelings of unworthiness
   - feeling alone and unsupported
5) If you're struggling to practice *forgiveness* as taught by the *Course*
   and shared in this book
6) It can also be used anytime after reading the *Forgiveness Prayer*
   to help you better understand and embody the deeper meaning as opposed to simply focusing on the words.

The meditative style of this process is intended to allow you to go beyond the form of the words of this *Prayer* to the meaning behind the words. In this way, you let go the idea of *"prayer"* as a series of words that you say and center in the idea of what it *means* to pray so you literally join your mind with God's.

A very effective way to use this is any time you are about to practice the **5 Step Forgiveness Process** so that you approach each step with a receptive frame of mind.

This process only takes about 5 minutes, but initially give yourself about 15 minutes, 5 minutes to get comfortable and relaxed, seated or lying down, in a place where you will be undisturbed. 5 minutes to experience the guided process, 5 minutes before you move on with your day, centered in your new perspective.

You can start by using this Process to change your state of mind as needed, until it automatically becomes your chosen way of being in every moment.

THE FORGIVENESS PRAYER

Forgive us our illusions, Father, and help us to accept our true relationship with You, in which there are no illusions, and where none can ever enter.

Our holiness is Yours.
What can there be in us that needs forgiveness when Yours is perfect?

The sleep of forgetfulness is only our (the) unwillingness to accept (remember) Your forgiveness and Your Love.

Let us not wander into temptation, for the temptation of the Son of God is not Your Will.

And let us accept only what You have given, and receive but this
into the minds which You created and which You love.
Amen.
T-16. VII.12:1-7

THE FORGIVENESS PRAYER MEDITATIVE PROCESS

*Let me realize that all of that appears to be taking place in
a world
outside me is the effect and reflection of my belief in
separation.*

*Let me be aware that what I think, how I feel about, and
the way
I respond to any situation, is based solely on my
perception
and not caused by the situation.*

*Let me be aware that everything happens in the mind.
That everything that appears in form, including my body
and the bodies of other people are illusory projections
from within the mind;
And in and of themselves they don't exist they have no
power
they are all simply illusions.*

*As I recognize all things as illusions I realize that nothing
or no one
can change or affect me, disempower or weaken me;
make me happy or unhappy.
And as I recognize and acknowledge all these things as
illusions I set
myself free.*

*Let me be willing to let go of believing in the illusion of
being a
separate body with a separate mind living in a world of
separation;
And let me accept the truth that I remain forever as I was
created to*

be, and I remain forever where I always am in the mind of God.

Let me be willing to accept that what I am is an aspect of God.
That my true nature is an extension and expression of God nothing
other than a "place" where God is expressing Itself in form.

In this awareness I am free remembering that I remain forever,
as I was created to be.

EPILOGUE: Your Invitation

Dear Forgiveness Partner,

I hope by now, being addressed as *"Forgiveness Partner"* is no longer a mystery. I opened with the promise of answering all your questions about this, and the radically different perspective of *forgiveness* that leads me to address you this way.

I hope I've fulfilled my promise!

What I have shared in the pages of this book is based on my personal understanding and experience of studying, teaching and practicing the Teachings of *A Course in Miracles* for over 15 years.

A Course in Miracles is a course in truly *"forgiving or letting go of"* the true cause of all guilt, pain, anger and resentment: your misperception of who you are, where you are, and what is taking place in every moment, situation or encounter.

I have shared this practice of *Course based Forgiveness* with my coaching and counseling clients to help them completely let go of guilt and emotional pain and experience genuine intimacy in their relationships so they can experience more peaceful, authentic and fulfilling lives.

As an ACIM Teacher I share this practice with students to help them better understand what the *Course* is saying, and how to effectively apply the teachings in their everyday lives.

I don't know where you are on your Journey but if you've read this far, like Bill and Helen were *(the two people through whom the Course came)* and like I was, you, too, are most likely looking for *"another way"*.

You can trust that *True Forgiveness* is that *"other way"* as it has proven to bring peace and healing to my life and the lives of many others.

So if you have been struggling to *forgive* yourself or another, having difficulty letting go of a painful or troubling situation or would simply like to experience a more peaceful, authentic, happy and genuinely successful life — you now have two choices:

1) You can choose to continue to practice *Conventional Forgiveness* keeping yourself locked in a cycle of pain and fear, and continue with the elusive pursuit of peace, happiness and success, through different forms and activities in the world.

Or

2) You can *choose* to practice *True Forgiveness*. This book has introduced the perspective and the process, and I'll be happy to help you put it into practice.

So please feel free to reach out to me with any questions for help in practicing *True Forgiveness*, and about upcoming Courses, Workshops and Coaching Programs for Healing and Transformation. You can reach me at either of the following with the assurance that I'll respond to every request:

Jennifer@jennifermcsween.com
(514) 769 – 4713

I'd like to thank you for sharing a part of your Journey with me by reading this book, and invite you to let *True Forgiveness* guide you the rest of the way. I promise you that the only thing you can possibly lose is your pain!

Your Forgiveness Partner,

Jennifer McSween

APPENDIX

The following is a list of some of the key terms used in the Course and in this book and the symbolic or metaphorical meaning behind them.

A FEW KEY METAPHORICAL TERMS USED IN THIS BOOK

FORGIVENESS
The Course defines forgiveness as, "letting go of the belief in the power of illusions". Seeing past the illusory forms and recognizing the truth that lies behind. Forgiveness is recognizing and acknowledging the truth.

GOD
God, like everything else is an idea. It is the idea of the potential or possibility for anything to be. God is all there is and all that is real. God is synonymous with love. God can also be described as that which remains unchanged and unaffected by anything else because there is nothing else. God is the source and essence of all things.

GUILT
Guilt is the belief that an idea that is the opposite of God could be real. For example, the idea that a: Godless, Unjust, Insane, Lacking, and Tragic thought or idea exists (i.e. that the world, which is an illustration of the thought of guilt, is real).

HEALING
Healing is accepting the truth and engaging in right thinking or only entertaining right-mindedness, or accepting the Holy Spirit's thought system instead of ego's thought system.

HOLY SPIRIT
The Holy Spirit is neither a presence nor a separate entity. The Holy Spirit is another term for the truth.

IDEAS
Ideas are the contents of the mind. The Course says that, mind is all there is.

ILLUSION
The Course defines everything in form; everything that is experienced through any of the senses such as the world, the entire universe, our bodies – any and everything that is perceived as separate as illusory.

EGO
The ego is the idea that what you are is a separate, individualized body with your own distinct personality, feelings, and problems unique to only you.

FEAR
False – Evidence – Appearing – Real. Fear is accepting the perception of any circumstance condition or event that is unlike love, i.e. unreal and doesn't exist, as if it was real and feeling threatened by it in some way.

JUDGMENT
Judgment is the perception that things have value and meaning in and of themselves. To judge is to attempt to determine right from wrong and/or to take it upon yourself to declare what should or shouldn't be.

LOVE
To love is to allow, accept, include, and let all things be without judgment or conditions.

PERCEPTION

Perception is interpretation. It is not what you see, but what you tell yourself what you are seeing means. It's your interpretation.

REALITY

Reality, like Spirit, is the true state of all that is. It is changeless, eternal, and formless; without levels or boundaries. Reality is never affected and can never be affected by anything or anyone.

MIND

In ACIM, Mind, God, and Spirit are used interchangeably. Mind can be seen as God (awareness and consciousness), all that is, exists, or is real.

MIRACLE

Contrary to the perspective of the world, the Course does not define a miracle as a change in condition, but a change in perception. That change in perception is also brought about by a change in perspective.

PEACE

Peace is a state of mind in which you experience absolute freedom from, or absence of any fear of conflict, danger, guilt, lack, disease, or any form of unrest.

BODY (The)

The body is an idea in the mind. It can be seen as the first and most concrete form in which we experience the idea of separation.

SIN

The idea that something can have a negative effect or affect and change reality in some way, i.e. to attack God or truth.

SPIRIT
Spirit is the essence – the essential nonphysical nature of all that is/exists.

TRUTH
Truth is the opposite of illusion. Truth is constant. Like reality, it is changeless and cannot be affected by anything. Truth cannot be destroyed or attacked. It cannot be perceived, learned, nor believed. It can only be discovered and accepted. To discover truth, you must search out and recognize all illusions that interfere with your awareness and acceptance of it.

(THE) WORLD
The "world" is a metaphor for any idea that is set apart in your mind and seen as separate — having an individualized existence — and to which you are giving attention in any moment or situation.

The world in which we seem to exist is nothing but the reflection of the "idea of separation" in its truest form. All that seems to take place in and as the world and as your life is your experiencing the idea of separation in different forms.

REFERENCES

All references to *A Course in Miracles* are from the Second Edition, 1996. Published by the Foundation for Inner Peace.

References to *A Course in Miracles* correspond to the Text (T), Workbook (W), Manual for Teachers (M) and Clarification of Terms (T) used in the Second Edition. For example:

T-21.in.1:6-7 corresponds to TEXT, Chapter 21, Introduction, Paragraph 1, Lines 6 to 7

W-pI.190.5:1-6 corresponds to Workbook, Part I, Lesson 190, Paragraph 5, Lines1-6.

M-10.2:1 corresponds to Manual for Teachers, Question 10, Paragraph 2, Line 1.

C-4.2:1 corresponds to Clarification of Terms, Term 4,Paragraph2, Line 1.

ABOUT THE AUTHOR

Rev. Jennifer McSween is an Ordained Metaphysical Minister and a Pathways of Light Ordained Ministerial Counselor. For over 15 years she has been a practicing spiritual psychotherapist and *A Course In Miracles* (ACIM) coach and teacher. Her unique, metaphysical methods go far beyond traditional motivational and self-help techniques, helping people to shift their perception, so they can become empowered to heal and transform their lives.

She works exclusively with the principles of *A Course in Miracles* and taught and facilitated ACIM based courses and workshops, for 13 years at a Spiritual College in Montreal. She is the founder of The Centre For Spiritual Affairs, a virtual space that serves open-minded, spiritually oriented, mature professionals. Under the umbrella of The Centre For Spiritual Affairs Rev. Jennifer offers her spiritually based ministerial services, and metaphysically based practices for healing and transformation.

Rev. Jennifer is also the director of the Quebec Division of the Canadian International Metaphysical Ministry (CIMM), an organization dedicated to improving the quality of life through the practice of metaphysical philosophy. She lives in Montreal Canada with her husband and daughter.

True Forgiveness is her first book and the platform for a series of related courses, workshops and programs, to be created over the coming year. To be notified when these life-transforming services become available, visit http://www.JenniferMcSween.com

"A HUMBLE REQUEST"

Thank You For Reading My Book!

I really appreciate all of your feedback, and I love hearing what you have to say.

This book is a platform for developing products programs and services for helping you meet your needs, for more peace healing and happiness in your life. I need your input so I can better understand how I can help you meet those needs.

Please leave me a helpful review on Amazon letting me know your thoughts and feelings about this book.

With gratitude, appreciation & much love!
Jennifer

Made in the USA
Las Vegas, NV
14 November 2020